Decisions

Decisions

The Complexities of Individual and Organizational Decision-Making

Karin Brunsson

Associate Professor, Uppsala University, Sweden

Nils Brunsson

Professor, Uppsala University, Sweden

 Edward Elgar
PUBLISHING

Cheltenham, UK • Northampton, MA, USA

Published by
Edward Elgar Publishing Limited
The Lypiatts
15 Lansdown Road
Cheltenham
Glos GL50 2JA
UK

Edward Elgar Publishing, Inc.
William Pratt House
9 Dewey Court
Northampton
Massachusetts 01060
USA

A catalogue record for this book
is available from the British Library

Library of Congress Control Number: 2017950442

This book is available electronically in the **Elgar**online
Business subject collection
DOI 10.4337/9781788110396

ISBN 978 1 78811 038 9 (cased)
ISBN 978 1 78811 040 2 (paperback)
ISBN 978 1 78811 039 6 (eBook)

Typeset by Columns Design XML Ltd, Reading
Printed and bound in Great Britain by TJ International Ltd, Padstow

Contents

About the authors

Karin Brunsson is Associate Professor of business administration. She teaches management accounting and control at Uppsala University and Jönköping International Business School. Her main interests concern the development of management ideas. In particular, she assessed the immense influence of Henri Fayol (see *The Notion of General Management*, 2007 and *The Teachings of Management, Perceptions in a Society of Organizations*, 2017). Her recent articles include 'Organizational Change in Intrusive and Non-Intrusive Environments' (2016), 'A dual perspective on management' (2016) and 'Regulating Interest-Free Banking' (2017).

Nils Brunsson is Professor of management and affiliated to Uppsala University and Score (Stockholm Centre for Organizational Research) at the Stockholm School of Economics and Stockholm University, Sweden. He has held chairs in management at the Stockholm School of Economics and at Uppsala University. Brunsson has published almost 30 books in the field of management and organization studies, including *The Irrational Organization, The Organization of Hypocrisy, Mechanisms of Hope, The Consequences of Decision-Making, A World of Standards, Reform as Routine* and *Meta-organizations* as well as numerous articles. He has studied organizational decision-making, administrative reform and standardization. His current research interests include the organization of markets, partial organization, meta-organizations and the social construction of competition. Brunsson has received several awards for his research and teaching and he is an honorary member of the European Group for Organization Studies (EGOS).

The quake

On Boxing Day, 2004 – Sunday, December 26 at 07:59 local time (01:59 Swedish time) – an earthquake hit just north of the island of Simeulue, Indonesia, about 160 km off the west coast of Sumatra. The magnitude of the quake, the epicentre of which was about 30 km below sea level, has been estimated at 9.0 on the Richter scale – at a minimum. Several km^3 of water were pushed up, and gargantuan waves swept the coasts. An estimated 250,000 people died in the tsunami.

Between 20,000 and 30,000 Swedes were in Thailand and Sri Lanka on this Boxing Day holiday. According to the Swedish Constitution, the task for Sweden's Prime Minister Göran Persson was to govern the country. What was his responsibility in a situation like this? What decisions did he and his staff make? What were the consequences of their decisions?

Swedish Radio reported the earthquake in its *Eko* broadcast at 04:00 and speculated that thousands of people might have been injured. About half an hour later, the Swedish Embassy in Bangkok telephoned the duty officer at the Ministry for Foreign Affairs, and they agreed that as many as 30,000 Swedish tourists could be in the area. The Swedish police were alerted a little before 06:00, the Rescue Services Agency at 07:30, and the prime minister about 07:45.

Discussions were ongoing Boxing Day afternoon among various units of the government offices and the Rescue Services Agency, concerning emergency response to assist Swedish travellers to Thailand. By that evening, the Board of Health and Welfare was involved. The Swedish Embassy in Bangkok sent a query about evacuation flights. But it was unclear who could make such a decision in this situation, and no decision was made.

The decision was delayed for so long that an emergency response force from the Rescue Services Agency was unable to depart for Thailand until the evening of December 28. By that time, the Thai

Ministry of Foreign Affairs had declared that it would gratefully accept help from the rest of the world. The Swedish response force soon proved to be under-resourced, and the Rescue Services Agency decided to send more personnel. Two additional teams left for Thailand, the first on December 30, the second on January 3. Flights taking travellers home began on December 29. The belated response had an adverse impact on both foreign and Thai citizens, who received poorer medical care or died as a result of over-crowded hospitals and overstretched medical personnel.

In a later inquiry into the course of events (SOU 2005:104), the Swedish government offices were criticized for their lack of an effective disaster management organization. Managers with the authority to make decisions that could be executed immediately were nowhere to be found. Responses took on the nature of improvisations.

The situation was unquestionably different in Italy, where a central disaster management unit of the Ministry of Foreign Affairs immediately decided to requisition aircraft and equipment for the urgently needed evacuations. Rescue equipment and medical personnel were on the way by the evening of Boxing Day. Evacuations of some 8,000 Italian tourists began on the evening of December 27.

* * *

When disasters and emergencies of various kinds occur, the importance of *decisions* becomes apparent. Those with the courage to make critical decisions can save lives.

But decision-making is a mundane activity – something everyone is involved in daily. And of no lesser importance is the fact that decisions are the stuff of life to organizations.

In this book, we examine the concept of decisions and describe the process of decision-making by individuals and organizations. We further describe the consequences of decisions and the complications inherent in decision-making – for individuals and organizations alike. At the end of the book, we return to the matter of decision-making by Swedish authorities after the tsunami disaster.

1. Decisions

The word *decision*, says the *Oxford English Dictionary* (2017), has French–Latin origins. From the 15th to the 18th century, it was used to denote something that had been separated from a larger thing or amount: a fragment or small piece, or the action of cutting something off:

> From rocks and stones along the sea continually, washed and dashed with the waves, therebe decisions passe of some parcels and small fragments. (1603)

> Human generation ... is performed by derivation or decision of part of the substance of the Parent. (1659)

At least from the 15th century, the word 'decision' could also define something more abstract – bringing a contest or a controversy to an end:

> After gret prossesse finished, and þe ful decision of many gret causes and quarales þat wer moved. (1413)

> For the decision of questions daily arising. (1833)

More specifically, 'decision' means the process of arriving at a conclusion regarding a matter under consideration or the result of this process:

> Fyrst they treated of Religion, and after muche decision, a decree was made ... (1560)

> The decisions of Judges ... are made the standing Rules. (1710)

Finally, decision denotes determination, resolve, and decidedness of character:

'Oh, Vere is not going for weeks – weeks,' declared Mrs. Jock with great decision. (1891)

The dictionary provides examples of compounds prefixed by the word 'decision': decision-making, decision-taking, decision method, decision procedure, decision rule, decision theory, and so on. Readers are probably convinced that decision is an important and frequently used concept, but how important? When and where are decisions made? Who makes decisions and why? And – not least – how do they go about it?

On the following pages, we answer these questions by making them more complicated than their mere definition permits. We hope that this endeavour will clarify some of the intriguing issues facing decision makers.

DECISIONS AND DECISION MAKERS

Many scholars see decision as equivalent to choice, a perception that concurs with the common understanding of the word. People who say that they have made a decision usually make it clear that not only have they chosen something, but that they thought about it beforehand and understood that they could have done it in another way or done something else entirely. They chose one of two or several possible ways. First thought, then decision. They use this meaning of 'decision', irrespective of whether they refer to a particular decision or to the general notion of decisions, and irrespective of whether the decision was made on behalf of them or on behalf of an organization.

In modern society, people are expected to be autonomous individuals with the right and the duty to decide on significant aspects of their lives. They are probably considerably more likely than people in earlier generations to regard themselves as decision makers. And in many situations, at least in the wealthier parts of the world, people have ample opportunity to choose among several options. They must determine what they do and do not want to do: They must make decisions.

When *individuals* make decisions about their own actions, they are essentially making a deal with themselves – although they may, of course, consult family members, friends or knowledgeable experts. After concluding their mental deliberations, they turn their attention to acting according to their decision – or to something else entirely.

Decisions in *organizations* are central, often critical, activities (Luhmann 2000; March and Simon [1958]1993). States, business firms, voluntary associations, and parts of these organizations – government agencies, subsidiaries, or departments – have managers or other people whose principal task is to make decisions about what other organization members shall do. Some parts of organizations specialize in decision-making and do little else: parliaments, municipal assemblies and the annual general meetings of corporations and voluntary associations, for example.

Decisions are also vital in *markets*, where individuals and organizations are expected to choose with whom they will do business and the goods or services these transactions will cover. When there is competition among sellers, buyers must choose among similar goods or services from equivalent suppliers, who may try to make their products difficult to compare by communicating a particular image or profile.

Decisions and Other Activities

Decisions are generally perceived as explanations of human behaviour. It is not surprising, therefore, that scholars in several social science disciplines are preoccupied with decisions. Social psychologists study individual decision-making; political scientists show how political decisions are made and demonstrate the effects of those decisions; students of organizations study how and why decisions are made in organizations, and the role these decisions play in the operations of organizations; and economists study decision-making in market contexts.

Decisions have become such a dominant idea that some people are led to believe that decisions precede all types of activities (or inactivity). But that assumption is not particularly useful for an analysis of decision-making. If decision and action are treated as synonymous, decisions become uninteresting. The question of how and why individuals and organizations make decisions, then, means the same as the question of why they act as they do. Answering that question here would be an overwhelming task, equal to describing the concerns of virtually all the social sciences.

We regard decisions as a particular activity, which, although certainly common, is not something that people are constantly engaged in. Many actions are undertaken without any decisions being made. And decisions do not necessarily lead to action. Yet, many decisions are made in many human contexts – which is why decisions are interesting! Consequently, it is important to try to understand when and how decisions are made, whether or not they lead to action and what other consequences they may have. These are the questions we address in this book.

We present a selection of thought-provoking (we think) ideas and results from studies of decisions and decision-making. We believe that people who want to understand their own decisions and those of others should be familiar with these ideas.

DECISIONS, ROUTINES AND INSTITUTIONS

People often act reflexively – without making a decision – as when jerking a hand away from a hot stove or squinting in strong sunlight. But there are other, more complex situations in which decisions do not precede action.

Ilya Ilyich Oblomov, the main character of Ivan Goncharov's novel *Oblomov* (Goncharov [1859]2014), has a hard time getting out of bed. Even though he has businesses to attend to, he usually lies there like a slug. Only rarely does he manage to make the decision to get up.

Obviously, this is unusual behaviour for a thirty-two-year-old man. Most people that age have established routines, and need give no thought to their morning activities. Getting up, eating breakfast, and brushing teeth involve no decision-making. They just do it. Likewise, organization members follow numerous routines in familiar situations. Organizations even decide on routines to be followed in the future, thereby reducing the need for future decisions. They introduce routine procedures for a range of situations – from handling customer complaints to salary negotiations.

People also tend to behave like others in their society in myriad contexts, without making decisions. Parents and teachers show or tell children and adolescents what is considered normal behaviour in various situations: adapting to others in everyday life, greeting others, buying food in a supermarket, or taking university classes.

As adults, they do not have to think about how they should behave or make decisions in every such situation. It is obvious to them that they should extend their right hand to greet another person, quietly join the queue at the supermarket checkout, or take a public seat in the lecture hall. Social scientists talk about how people act in concert with *social institutions*: patterns of behaviour that are taken for granted (Jepperson 1991).

Organizations can rely on social institutions in many situations. A university does not have to make and communicate the decision that students must sit in the public seats in the lecture halls. Students already know that. Business firms can presume that the people they employ are aware that they have managers who are entitled to make decisions about the tasks to be assigned to other employees.

Institutions promote predictability. People can trust that others greet them in a particular way, join the queue at the supermarket and sit where they should in a lecture hall. That business firms have managers is common knowledge. Without institutions, the social order would be endangered. People would be constantly making decisions about what they should do that precise moment, different people would make different decisions, and it would be difficult for others to predict the decisions that others were going to make. Were there no institutions, people would have to spend an inordinate amount of time interpreting and trying to understand how other people think. And every instance of cooperation and coordination would have to be preceded by deliberations and decisions. Institutions are highly practical. They make life easier because people do not have to devote every waking hour to making decisions.

FOUR LOGICS

When people *do* make decisions, how do they go about it? We distinguish four logics that they apply:

- *the logic of consequences*, which implies that decision makers try to assess the outcomes of various courses of action;
- *the logic of appropriateness*, which implies that decision makers consider the rules relevant to the current situation;
- *the logic of imitation*, which implies that decision makers try to imitate what they or others have done in the past; and

- *the logic of experimentation*, which implies that decision makers try to do something with little previous deliberation; rather, they focus on evaluating the results in retrospect, in order to determine whether they should continue along the same lines or take a novel approach.

We discuss each of the four logics in the following sections.

The Logic of Consequences

Decision makers who apply the logic of consequences look ahead. They try to predict the action that will best satisfy them once the decision has been implemented. They consider their options for action and try to guess the outcomes of different options. They try to compare these predicted consequences with their general preferences – their values, goals, interests or tastes – then choose the action for which the consequences align most closely with their preferences.

Its future orientation makes the logic of consequences difficult to apply (March and Olsen 1989). The future is unknown, by definition, and the available options lie in the future, as do the consequences and preferences with which the options must be compared. This situation applies even to the immediate future, although the immediate future is often perceived as relatively certain. As Saint Paul said, long ago, 'For we know in part, and we prophecy in part/ … /For now we see through a glass, darkly …' (1 Corinthians 13: 9–12).

The Logic of Appropriateness

Decision makers who use the logic of appropriateness base their decisions on rules or norms and try to make decisions consistent with them. A court is an archetypal example of an organization that primarily applies this logic. The court's remit is to determine which legal rules should be applied in a particular case and how the rules should be interpreted in the situation at hand. Prosecutors and defence attorneys draw different conclusions about guilt and innocence and what sanctions should be meted out, but it is the court in the form of the judge or jury that decides. The logic of appropriateness implies that decision makers try to answer three elementary questions (March and Olsen 1989).

What kind of a person am I? Different rules apply to different people and to the same person, depending upon the role that person is assuming for the moment. The rules for parents are not the same as for their children. The rules for access to land are not the same for the owners of the land as they are for others. Various rules apply to different members of an organization. 'I' may also refer to an organization, and in that case other rules apply than those that apply to individuals – different state laws, for example. In addition, there are different rules for different types of organizations: Banks must comply with certain rules that do not apply to department stores, and different rules apply to corporations and sole proprietorships.

What kind of situation is this? Different rules apply in different situations. Trying to take a ball away from someone else is allowed in a football match, but not in a sporting goods store. People are allowed to use a certain type of violence in self-defence that is not permitted in other contexts. A company on the brink of insolvency must prepare a balance sheet for liquidation purposes.

What shall a person such as I do in a situation such as this? Decision makers who understand their role in a particular situation must take a stance on which rules they should follow. Even when they are aware of the rules, there are often several possible interpretations. In everyday life, it is usually easy to understand the rules that apply, but in situations that are infrequently encountered, people must deliberate more in order to arrive at a decision. Then they may need the help of lawyers or other compliance experts – experts in such diverse areas as accounting, etiquette or child rearing.

Although the rules that individuals and organizations follow may be contradictory and tricky to interpret, they must exist beforehand for a decision based on the logic of appropriateness to work. Decision makers applying the logic of appropriateness look backward rather than forward – to existing rules rather than possibilities that the future may bring. Looking backward often feels safer than trying to predict the unknown future, as required by the logic of consequences.

The Logic of Imitation

Like those who use the logic of appropriateness, decision makers
using imitation base their decisions on something that already
happened. They consider what others have done and ride on the
coattails of previously successful investors when deciding what
stocks to buy; they imitate close friends for all sorts of shopping
and child-rearing decisions. Imitation is one of several methods for
learning a profession or trade; future doctors, teachers and carpen-
ters learn by observation how experienced practitioners work, and
future auditors are introduced to the profession through comprehensive internships.

Organizations also imitate each other; they may develop products
similar to a competitor's, market themselves the same way others
do, or organize and manage operations the same way they believe
others do.

But neither individuals nor organizations want to imitate just
anyone. They follow the lead of their peers – those they believe to
belong to the same category as they do (Strang and Meyer 1993).
When deciding on clothes, men and women tend to imitate members of their own sex; professionals imitate the style of people
within their profession. Universities imitate other universities – or
they consider themselves as primarily belonging to a more general
category such as organizations and imitate other organizations –
business firms, for instance (Brunsson and Sahlin-Andersson 2000).
And individuals and organizations may imitate themselves; they
reflect on what they did in a similar situation in the past and try to
do likewise (Sevón 1996).

The Logic of Experimentation

The logics we have discussed so far presume that decision makers
think first and act later. People who apply the logic of experimentation do almost the opposite: They deliberate more after they act
than they did before. Without giving much thought to which action
is best, they do something and then evaluate the results. If they are
happy with the outcome, they are able to wash their hands of
further decision-making. If they are unhappy, they make a new
decision. The new decision may (but need not) be designed as an
experiment, which means that the procedure is repeated.

Instead of trying to guess what will happen after a decision has been made, which those who use the logic of consequences try to do, decision makers who experiment take an empirical stance: Instead of guessing their preferences, they discover which preferences they arrive at if they act in a particular way. Rather than guessing the consequences, they create consequences. Like imitation or rule following, experimentation is based on historical information. The difference is that the decision makers produce this information themselves. Action is not only the result of decisions; decisions are also the result of action.

People may be thinking according to the logic of experimentation when they choose an educational path. It is difficult to know in advance what is included in a programme of study. One way to find out is to begin a course and see if it is of interest. Those who find it interesting enrol in the advanced course as well; those who do not, enrol in a different course.

Organizations apply the logic of experimentation when they decide to launch a new product in selected markets, in order to discover the existing demand or to launch different versions of the same product in different areas. The success of Japanese companies in the 1980s was ascribed to their use of experimentation. Instead of predicting the consequences of various levels of inventory, in order to determine the optimal level, they reduced costly intermediate inventories, observed what happened, tried to correct the problems that arose, and then further reduced inventories. Inventories and inventory costs turned out to be smaller for Japanese than for US companies, which had calculated the 'optimal' size in advance (Masaaki 1986).

The Logics Intertwine

The four logics are simplifications, useful for analysing and understanding a complex reality. In practice, they often exist in combinations. Rules can be (but are not necessarily) designed according to the logic of consequences: What would the effects of other rules be? People can follow the same logic when they choose among different rules: Which rule seems to produce the best outcome? Those who want to imitate may try to formulate a rule that describes how others have behaved and follow that rule. The experimental decision maker may begin by trying to act in a manner that resembles how another successful person or organization has acted.

Last but not least, there are rules for the way decisions should be made according to the logic of consequences – rules for the way rational decisions are made. Somewhat paradoxically, decision makers who follow these rules apply the logic of appropriateness in order to improve their use of the logic of consequences.

RATIONAL DECISIONS

Depending on the situation and the decision maker, all four logics discussed here are more or less reasonable. For organizations (and perhaps, to an increasing extent, for individuals), the logic of consequences is the decision logic most widely accepted, however. An extreme form of this logic is the idea of rationality. As demonstrated in this section, rationality includes much-discussed, though unfeasible, expectations of decision makers.

When people discuss decisions, they tend to come back to the term 'rationality', which may be used in connection with all four logics. What is perceived as rational then becomes generally understood as reasonable, even intelligent. In this book, we use a narrower and therefore more useful definition of rationality related but not identical to sociologist Max Weber's ([1924]1964) means–end rationality (*Zweckrationalität*). In our interpretation, rationality means three things: Decisions should precede action; decisions should be made according to the logic of consequences; deliberations should be made in a particular, highly systematic way. Being rational does not imply merely guessing about the future in general; any guess should proceed in a particular way and be consistent with the rules of the 'model of rational decision-making' (Simon [1957]1965). We refer to this model when we discuss 'rational' and 'rationality'.

- Decision makers should not only clarify their preferences; they should also rank the preferences according to their preference function – which means that they should realize how important each preference is in relation to all others.
- Decision makers should examine *all* conceivable options; otherwise, they risk missing the best option.

- Decision makers should examine *all* consequences relevant to their preferences; otherwise, they run the risk of misjudging their options and choosing the wrong one.
- Decision makers should be able to use their preference function to compare *all* conceivable consequences with their various preferences. Options and consequences must not influence their preferences. Should decision makers spontaneously feel inclined to choose a particular option, they are not allowed to adjust their preferences to fit that option.
- Decision makers should think not only about the immediate future, but also about the entire future in which they expect their decision to have consequences.

With this use of the term 'rational', it is clear that the other logics are neither rational nor irrational – but rather 'a-rational'. Although the concept of rationality does not apply to them, other logics are as *reasonable* as the logic of consequences and the idea of rationality; they merely represent other forms of intelligence.

The model of rational decision-making has at least one argument in its favour: It should guarantee that the decision maker chooses the option that is likely to result in the most positive consequences. But the challenges for people who try to make rational decisions pile up. If they do not successfully overcome all those challenges, there are no guarantees that the decision will be the right one.

Problematic Preferences

It is easier to be rational if one has stable preferences. But it is common knowledge that preferences may change over time as people discover what others like or how they behave or when they see the consequences of their decisions.

> How can I know who I am until I see what they do?

> How can I know what we did until I see what we produced? (Weick 1995, pp. 23, 30)

It is difficult to predict preferences (March 1987). But it is, after all, their future preferences that will determine if decision makers are satisfied with a particular action. A common breach of the model of rational decision-making is that decision makers proceed from their current preferences, without giving the matter much thought – even in situations in which it is likely that these preferences have changed by the time the consequences of the action become apparent. By the time this happens, decision makers may want something other than what they wanted when they made their decisions.

Methods for predicting preferences are in short supply. One way out of this dilemma is to try to imitate the preferences of more experienced individuals. Young people may imitate the preferences of their parents, for instance, rather than basing their decision on their current preferences. Other than that, and somewhat ironically, there is only one clear decision rule: People who have good reason to assume that their preferences will change, but do not know how they will change, should not proceed from current preferences. They should not do what they feel like doing at the moment. But this rule is not precise; it offers no guidance on how to choose among all the options that one does not like.

Decisions already made or actions already taken may influence preferences. The decision to take a particular action, like the action itself, may mean that one begins to like what one is doing. 'Positive endogenous preferences', means that the preferences accommodate to whatever is happening (March 1978), making it easier to follow the logic of consequences – because any decision or action becomes satisfactory. Take the example of higher education: Professionals may come to believe that what they have learnt as students is important, making almost everyone happy with their choice of education. Those who trust that this will be the case need not think very hard about which programme they should apply to; they can expect to be satisfied, no matter which educational path they choose. Similarly, few people regret that they decided to become parents once the baby has arrived. Thus it is much more likely that one is satisfied with the decision to have children than the opposite decision – thus strongly facilitating the decision.

Unfortunately, the opposite may also apply: Decision makers' preferences may adapt to their decisions in such a way that they come to dislike what they have decided. With 'negatively endogenous preferences', they become dissatisfied, regardless of the options they choose. In and of itself, this situation also facilitates decision-making, but it has few advantages beyond that one. If the grass is always greener on the other side of the fence, it does not matter what decision is made; the decision maker will be unhappy either way. Ranking and weighing preferences is another pitfall of the model of rational decision-making. How important is one preference over the others? People who believe it is crucial that motorists can move quickly from Point A to Point B must weigh time savings against the risk that high speed may cause more injuries or fatalities in road traffic accidents – which no one thinks is good. One needs a measure for comparing these fundamentally different preferences. Yet the person who does not have that type of preference function but thinks that these values are immensurable may get into serious trouble when trying to apply the model of rational decision-making. The problem is multiplied when several people must make a joint decision: There is no obviously correct method for balancing the preferences of different people.

Problematic Projections

Assessments of options and consequences must also be based on projections that are almost always uncertain, especially if the decisions refer to actions in the distant future or if long-term consequences can be foreseen. It is difficult to know the consequences of different options. One can certainly calculate the aggregate expected value of a decision by multiplying the probability of various outcomes by the benefit that various outcomes are expected to produce. But if there are no statistically calculated probabilities for various outcomes, decision makers are forced to rely on estimates – subjective probabilities. This is the case when business firms and government agencies make risk assessments by estimating the threats to the organization and the probability that these threats occur. These probabilities are similar uncertain future assessments, however, and the problem of the uncertain future remains.

It is difficult to be aware of all options – of every possibility. The risk here is a lack of imagination. Perhaps the successful entrepreneur is the person who happened to spot a highly favourable option that had escaped the notice of everyone else.

Information gathering is rarely free; it can be both arduous and time-consuming and can impinge upon the decision maker's opportunities to address other key issues. When many problematic, time-consuming and costly forecasts and deliberations are required of decision makers, they may find it rational to make a decision about the decision. In principle, it should be possible to start by making a rational decision about how much time is worthwhile to spend on making a rational decision. But how much time should then be spent on the preparatory decision? A rational decision can also be made about that – at the peril of the decision maker becoming stuck in a never-ending spiral of rational decisions.

The pitfalls of following the model of rational decision-making are one reason why both individuals and organizations simplify. They may still aspire to be rational, but they realize that they do not have the unlimited capacity to gather and analyse information. Instead, people consider the information available and base their decision on their present preferences. They evaluate a limited number of options and find an option that may not be the best one, but one that they believe is good enough: Instead of optimizing, as the model of rational decision-making presumes, they reduce the number of options evaluated by *satisficing* (Simon 1955).

Some people give up in the face of these difficulties and use another logic that seems easier. Once a decision has been made, however, the situation changes. Individuals and organizations that engage in post-hoc rationalization revert to the logic-of-consequence thinking and that of rationality.

POST-HOC RATIONALIZATION

Thus far, we have addressed various modes of reasoning – different logics – in connection with decision-making. But after a decision has been made, decision makers who justify their decisions must not necessarily refer to the logic they applied when making the decision. Under many circumstances, they are expected to justify their decisions in line with the logic of consequences, preferably in a version that is as rational as possible. Many people undergo post-hoc rationalizing after making a decision.

Following rules within the logic of appropriateness rarely elicits admiration, at least not if the rules of appropriateness were drafted by others. So justifying decisions by saying that 'I simply followed the rules' is rarely acceptable. Even people who decide on new rules are often forced to rationalize them: They must demonstrate that the rules are motivated by their positive consequences, and they are not installed merely to satisfy the decision makers' whim or emotionally laden prejudice.

Imitation is a similarly low-status approach. Justifying decisions by saying that 'I did what everyone else does' is as bad as or worse than merely following rules. Experimentation, on the other hand, may seem bold and innovative, at least to those who like the decision. But few, if any, decision makers talk about experimentation when their decisions proved to have disastrous consequences; to do so would make them appear careless.

In modern society, it is even more difficult to justify decisions by referring to tradition, the will of God, or some superstitious belief (Weber [1924]1964). And it is rarely a valid explanation to claim that the decision was made on impulse or by following gut feelings. Instead, ever-wider areas of life are rationalized, including leisure time and family life. Even holidays serve a purpose: People claim that they decided to spend their vacation in a certain way by arguing that they must learn to play golf, recharge their batteries, or get a tan. And if further interrogated, they are expected to come up with a relatively rational explanation why they chose a particular way of reaching their purpose.

Even the decision to marry a particular person may today require sophisticated post-hoc rationalization. Back in 1975, when the King of Sweden explained to journalists why he had proposed to Silvia Sommerlath, he could refer to his emotions rather than to any form of rationality: 'It just said click!' (YouTube 2013a). Thirty-three years later, when his daughter, Crown Princess Victoria, became engaged to Daniel Westling, she gave the long, pensive explanation that their 'love grew gradually' over seven years of acquaintance, when she found out that they had 'a perfect personal chemistry' (YouTube 2013b). The Crown Princess gave the impression of having examined her preferences and possible options. But perhaps she simply adapted to the recent but strong expectation for post-hoc rationalization – even of love affairs.

Whereas individuals sometimes get away with references to their emotions or their prejudices, the demands for post-hoc rationalization remain high in organizations. Post-hoc rationalization has become a key task for executives, heads of government agencies, board chairmen and the burgeoning cadre of information officers. In fact, organizations are impregnated with arguments based on the logic of consequences and rationality – even when these forms of intelligence do not govern their decision-making. Through post-hoc rationalization, decision processes that have proceeded in various ways are described as complying with the model of rational decision-making. Thus outsiders – and perhaps the decision makers themselves – are led to believe that rationality is a more common form of decision-making than is actually the case, thereby reinforcing the general tendency to perceive rationality as a worthy and feasible pursuit.

2. Individuals as decision makers

One hundred years ago, management consultant and writer Mary Parker Follett ([1918]1998) questioned the notion of individuals as separate entities. This was a 19th century idea, Follett maintained, emphasizing the interaction between individuals and society. Twenty years later, sociologist Norbert Elias ([1939]2000) argued along the same lines: Is it even possible to distinguish between the individual and society? The notion that people are individuals who can function independently is 'an artificial product', wrote Elias (p. 481).

Follett and Elias proceeded from the conviction that individuals and societies develop in a reciprocal relationship of dependency. In their view, humans are first of all social beings. But old beliefs about individuals as separate, unique beings have proven persistent and seem, if anything, to be gaining ascendancy. Few people think of individuals as artificial products any more. On the contrary, there are countless signs that people are regarded – and see themselves – primarily as individuals, and that it is considered both natural and self-evident to do so. 'Everyone has the right to be treated as an individual', proclaimed a headline in the Swedish daily newspaper *Dagens Nyheter* (2013a).

The perspective on people as individuals parallels the view – and self-identification – of people as decision makers. When people are seen as individuals, they are no longer passive victims of circumstance; on the contrary, they should decide for themselves how they want to arrange their lives and make decisions in a wide variety of areas: selecting schools, healthcare providers, pension funds, electricity suppliers, telephone companies, educational programmes and careers.

In wealthy societies, where advertising plays a prominent role, people increasingly find themselves in decision-making situations. As individuals, they are encouraged to find 'their right and true selves' by deciding to buy specific products, whether cars, watches, mobile phones or handbags (Fournier 1998). Many advertisements communicate the idea that deep down people have a core of genuine and immutable identity that they should discover and express. 'Today, I am my true self', explains a young woman, who lost 40 kilos and is advertising for a slimming company (*Dagens Nyheter* 2013b). 'I have become the Helena I was from the start', says actress Helena af Sandeberg in an interview (*Dagens Nyheter* 2013c). There is also a large genre of confessional fiction informed by assertiveness and 'a unique self-image', and that genre seems to be growing (Elam 2012, p. 12).

This development is reflected by linguistic changes. People use the expression 'chose to' in every imaginable, inappropriate or even impossible context, so frequently that it is on the verge of becoming meaningless filler.

> 'After the scandal, he chose to resign.'
> 'We chose to interview Director P.'
> 'I chose to buy herring for lunch.'
> 'I choose to believe in miracles.'

Authors of popular self-help books encourage individuals to practice decision-making in virtually every area of life (for example, Duhigg 2016). And Weight Watchers once announced that losing weight is not primarily a question of eating less or getting more exercise; most important is to make 'smart choices'.

Decision-making then consumes a great deal of a person's life. At worst, life itself becomes a project, which individuals control and realize by consistently making decisions in line with their project goals (Beckman 1983; Berger et al. 1974; Frykman 1988).

According to a popular, contemporary version of rationality, one should state one's preferences as 'goals', 'targets' or clear and explicit ambitions. It is no longer enough to like some things and dislike others; there is a desirable future state of affairs that can be achieved only through concerted effort. Preferences expressed as goals or targets connect to the idea of life as a project.

Not everyone is always eager to make decisions, however. Uncertain decision makers tend to postpone their resolution. They prefer to wait and see. Perhaps some difficult question will resolve itself, if only they have patience and do not act hastily. Or they adopt a blithe attitude and convince themselves that the matter is unworthy of too much attention – as in the Swedish province of Värmland, where the saying goes: 'It will all work out! And if it doesn't work out, so what?'

People can talk themselves into the idea that there is no choice and no question of any decision – they simply have to do what they are about to do. Many such instances relate to consumption. It is relatively easy to convince oneself that new winter shoes or an updated mobile phone are necessities. Maybe life becomes easier that way:

> *La plus belle vie possible m'a toujours paru être celle où tout est déterminé soit par la contrainte des circonstances soit par de telles impulsions, et où il n'y a jamais place pour aucun choix.* (Weil 1957, p. 33)

> The most beautiful life possible has always seemed to me to be one where everything is determined, either by the pressure of circumstances or by impulses, and where there is never any room for choice.

But when people *do* make decisions, how do they go about it? Do they use the logic of consequences or the logic of appropriateness? Do they make their decisions by imitating, or do they experiment, arriving at the decision by trial and error? Or are there other forms of decision-making that do not fit any of these categories? In the rest of this chapter, we discuss some intricacies of the different decision logics.

We begin with the logic of consequences, which – especially its rational form – derives its high status from the fact that it concurs with the notion of the independent individual. Rational decisions are based on preferences, which reside within the individuals. A rational decision process should guarantee that individuals choose the actions that best fulfil their own, inner desires; they control the future by adapting it to their own wishes; at least this is the general presumption. The logics of appropriateness and imitation are accorded lower status because they do not presume separate and unique individuals; rather they run contrary to such notions. Those who comply with rules designed by others demonstrate that they are not in control. And those who imitate demonstrate their dependence rather than their independence. The logic of experimentation does not directly conflict with the notion of individuals; but nor does it confirm it, as the logic of rationality does.

PROBLEMS OF RATIONAL DECISION-MAKING

Attempts to apply the logic of consequences – and behave rationally – is not a new phenomenon. US scientist and politician Benjamin Franklin reasoned along rational lines, when, in the second half of the 18th century, he designed a method of systematic argumentation. Franklin, who claimed he had created a 'moral algebra', suggested that a person faced with the task of making a decision should evaluate two alternatives by dividing a piece of paper into two columns, headed *Pro* and *Con*, under which arguments for and against should be categorized. When a pro argument and a con argument seemed equal, both were stricken. Two pro reasons could be considered equal to three con reasons, and all five stricken. If, after a day or two of further consideration, nothing new of importance occurs on either side, the decision maker could come to a determination accordingly (Gigerenzer and Goldstein 1999).

'I have found great advantage from this kind of equation', wrote Franklin in 1772 in a letter to British scientist Joseph Priestley. Franklin emphasized that his method gave him an overview and time to think and that he was less likely to take a rash step. The procedure he recommended seems complicated and time-consuming, however. It is based on the expectation that people are to make a number of difficult judgements – in practice, to make several small decisions – before arriving at their final determination. The question then becomes how useful Franklin's rule really is. Certainly not everyone wants to go to the trouble of finding preferences, information and options. Some people argue like the Swedish poet who preferred to live in a world only loosely connected to reality (Lillpers 2012, p. 66, translated from Swedish):

… we
who believe we can make wise decisions
without facts
have no interest in the kind of reality
that makes things harder.

In practice, people simplify their decision-making in a variety of ways. The following sections include examples of so-called heuristics (rules of thumb, simplifications) that are frequently used and certainly facilitate decision-making.

One Decision Criterion

Even those who make an effort to choose by weighing all conceivable possibilities need to simplify the task of making decisions. They sidestep the rigorous demands of rationality. When biologist and theologian Charles Darwin pondered whether or not he should marry, he is said to have first tried to compare the advantages and disadvantages of marriage systematically, roughly as Benjamin Franklin had recommended. (See Box 2.1.)

BOX 2.1 DARWIN'S QUERY

MARRY	Not MARRY
Children – (if it please God) – constant companion, (friend in old age) who will feel interested in one, object to be beloved and played with – better than a dog anyhow – Home, and someone to take care of house – Charms of music and female chit-chat. These things good for one's health. Forced to visit and receive relations *but terrible loss of time.* My God, it is intolerable to think of spending one's whole life, like a neuter bee, working, working and nothing after all. – No, no won't do. – Imagine living all one's day solitarily in smoky dirty London House. – Only picture yourself a nice soft wife on a sofa with good fire, and books and music perhaps – compare this vision with the dingy reality of Grt Marlboro' St.	No children, (no second life) no one to care for one in old age. ... Freedom to go where one liked – Choice of Society and *little of it.* Conversation of clever men at clubs. – Not forced to visit relatives, and to bend in every trifle – to have the expense and anxiety of children – perhaps quarrelling. *Loss of time* – cannot read in the evenings – fatness and idleness – anxiety and responsibility – less money for books etc. – if many children forced to gain one's bread. – (But then it is very bad for one's health to work too much) Perhaps my wife won't like London; then the sentence is banishment and degradation with indolent idle fool –

Source: Reproduced from Gigerenzer and Todd (1999, pp. 7–8).

How did this list help Darwin make his decision? Could he really compare the advantages of a warm fire with the disadvantages of not being able to afford as many books? Could he even compare the joy of children with the anxiety and responsibility for the children that he simultaneously imagined? (As seen from his compilation, Darwin did not slavishly follow Franklin's rule; instead he made a jumble of pros and cons.)

Gigerenzer and Todd (1999), who recount Darwin's decision method, imagine that Darwin (who married his cousin and eventually fathered ten children) confined himself in practice to a single decision criterion: He compared the prospects of living alone in a dirty and smoky house in London with the scenario of *a soft wife on a sofa* – and suddenly had no difficulty making up his mind. Darwin did not need to conduct a complete analysis of all possible consequences of marriage, the scholars argue. A single criterion was enough for him to conclude his deliberations and enter the marriage.

Little Information

In many cases, people simplify their decision-making further by not gathering much information about the future; rather they proceed from the little information they happen to have available. They still think about the future (according to the logic of consequences), but begin with the present and base their decision on the information at hand (Kahneman 2011). Or their search for further information is limited, but they are ready to make a decision based on a few clues (Nisbett and Ross 1980). Chances are, however, that their decisions run contrary to their own best interests.

This happens in many mundane shopping situations, as in a grocery store handing out leaflets informing potential customers that it has reduced the price of a popular box of chocolates. Those who buy these boxes are led to believe they made a bargain, even though identical boxes are still cheaper with their regular grocers. Similarly, customers about to exit a hardware store find many bargains apart from the rake they originally meant to buy. (But if they never find out that they have purchased false bargains, they may still be happy shoppers.)

Once people have made up their minds, they typically find it difficult to change them, even if they later obtain information indicating that they were wrong. It is easier to give credence to information that confirms preconceived opinions than it is to accept information that conflicts with it (Nisbett and Ross 1980). A new and interesting acquaintance will remain interesting until there is overwhelming evidence to the contrary, and people who are disliked at first sight will have a difficult time proving that they are both interesting and attractive.

There are situations, however, in which limited and incomplete information leads to more accurate assessments. When asked which German cities are biggest, US students chose the cities they had heard of, and because large cities are mentioned in the media more often than other smaller towns, the students often gave the right answer. They were able to choose the largest German cities more accurately than they could identify the largest US cities, about which they had relatively better knowledge. And once the students had learnt more about German cities, their ability to identify the largest cities declined (Goldstein and Gigerenzer 1999).

The inclination to choose the familiar, combined with the idea that less information can lead to better choices, can be exploited when making decisions about buying or selling stock (Borges et al. 1999). Shares that are frequently mentioned in the media often demonstrate better price performance than less well-known shares do. Even if the companies have been targets of criticism, investors generally profit when they buy shares in companies that they recognize from media coverage; they can usually count on the share prices having already adjusted to the bad news – and are likely to rise again.

It is possible, therefore, that people with little information will make more accurate judgements and advantageous decisions than they would have, had they been knowledgeable about the matter. This applies in situations in which the limited information they have gathered provides sufficient guidance for a decision and when additional (but still limited) information tends to create confusion. In these cases, even superstition or urban legends can provide good guidance. One such urban legend claimed that rat parts had been found in pizzas (af Klintberg 1986). People who believed this message and refrained from eating unhealthy pizza probably acquired a healthier lifestyle as a consequence of a false premise.

Even information that is obviously wrong but agrees with some-body's wishful thinking – or prejudices – will be found plausible.

Many people allow themselves to be fooled by illusions. Even those who measured the two lines in Figure 2.1 – and *know* they are identical in length – find it difficult to liberate themselves from the perception that the bottom line is longer than the top line.

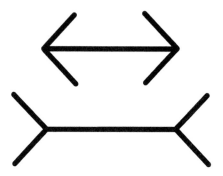

Source: Reproduced from Kahneman (2011, p. 27).

Figure 2.1   Two lines of the same length – or maybe not?

People who consider their own problems unique sometimes believe that they need no special information in order to make decisions (Kahneman and Lovallo 1993). They may daydream about how quickly they will be able to write a doctoral thesis or how beautiful they will be after cosmetic surgery, ignoring available information about how well others succeeded with similar projects. Had they used this information to guide their decisions, they would likely have been less optimistic – and perhaps decided not to write the thesis or undergo surgery.

Few Options

Decision-making is easier if the number of options considered is limited (Cyert and March [1963]1992; Simon 1955). Decision makers may limit their options by making one major, categorical decision. People who are looking for a new apartment decide that they do not want to live in the eastern part of the city; those who are going to buy a digital camera may decide on a certain brand, a certain price range or a minimum number of pixels.

Once the decision makers have identified an option they are relatively happy with, they can suspend their search for more options and make a decision. Because it proves to be difficult – or costly or time consuming – to find the best solution to some problem or to achieve exactly the target they set for themselves, they settle for a satisfactory solution. They may have to lower their aspirations, adapting their preferences to what proves to be feasible. Or they may adapt their preferences to one option. Those who fall in love with a new apartment, even though it does not have the two bathrooms they want, adjust their preferences by talking themselves into the advantage of a single bathroom: It makes cleaning easier.

Erratic Judgements

Decisions made hastily, with little information and without much effort may, in fact, be wrong decisions. An oft-cited example is the following simple maths exercise, to which many people impulsively (or overconfidently) give the wrong answer. Only when they take time to reflect do they realize their mistake (Kahneman 2011, p. 44).

A bat and ball cost $1.10.
The bat costs one dollar more than the ball.
How much does the ball cost?

Social psychologist Daniel Kahneman talks about 'mental short-cuts', explaining this behaviour by describing the dual nature of the human capacity to reason. People make decisions in two ways, Kahneman argues, using expressions borrowed from Stanovich and West (2000): System 1 and System 2.

System 1 is the system most often used. It functions emotionally, impulsively and quickly. It tends towards clarity, simplicity and order and leaves little room for thought or logical reasoning. This system never takes a break, but is working constantly. System 1 often kicks in when System 2 is busy with something effortful.

System 2 involves conscious thought and comparisons with individual preferences; it is oriented towards the use of relevant information to create conditions for well-founded conclusions and decisions that seem likely to produce the decision maker's desired outcome. Someone who wants to give a correct answer to the bat-and-ball problem must make an effort and use System 2 to figure out that the ball actually costs five cents, not ten, which is the usual answer from people who rely on System 1.

Because System 1 is easily accessible and requires little effort, people use this system to a much greater extent than they use System 2. Because System 2 takes some work and because people like to conserve their energy, they tend to use System 2 only in relation to particularly complex questions, like multiplying 17 by 24. Or they may use it for making decisions they consider especially important – like choosing among expensive goods: automobiles, washing machines or digital cameras.

There are ways of making System 2 questions into System 1 questions, however. One way is through substitution. When people are confronted with difficult issues that demand effortful deliberation, they tend to make things easier by answering a simpler question. Instead of considering the sacrifices that they are willing to make to save an endangered species, they picture *one* pitiful species, and answer the question based on how they feel when they see dying dolphins. When asked how happy they are with their lives, they recount their mood at the time (examples from Kahneman 2011, p. 98).

Faith

Faith seems as important in decision-making situations as it has proved to be in medical matters, where it is known as the placebo effect. People who *believe* they understand their situation are often better equipped for success than those who look more realistically – and pessimistically – at their predicament. They *do* something. They do not give up! And in many situations, action is better than passivity, even in cases of exaggerated optimism or when the decision makers misunderstand the information available to them (as in the case of writing a thesis).

People who mistake luck for skill draw conclusions about causal relationships that are irrelevant to the situation they face at the moment. They trust what they see as their experience and believe that they are more influential than they actually are. These decision makers become optimistic – even hyper-optimistic – on the wrong premises (Langer 1975; March 1994). But in certain situations, that is all for the best – and may even save lives.

The story of Hungarian soldiers camping in the Alps is an illustration of faith moving mountains. The soldiers were sent on a scouting mission and were taken by surprise by a blizzard. Their commander feared that he had sent his own soldiers to a certain death. Miraculously, however, they were able to make their way back to the camp alive. One of them had found a map in his pocket. The commander asked to see the map. It turned out that the soldiers had been following a map not of the Alps but of the Pyrenees (Holub 1977).

The Bible tells a similar story – but with a different outcome – in which St Peter, like Jesus, walks on the water (Matthew 14:22–33). Only when he is scared by the strong wind and loses faith, does Peter sink into the water.

THE LOGIC OF APPROPRIATENESS

People who apply the logic of appropriateness follow rules created by themselves or others. They follow different rules in different contexts, and many different rules in the course of an ordinary day. They typically follow traffic rules on the way to work, and once at work they follow rules about everything from the number of permitted coffee breaks to the hierarchical rules that require them to do what the boss tells them to do. When they stop at the supermarket on the way home, they follow rules about queuing and paying for the groceries they purchase, and then there are rules about how late they can arrive to collect their children from preschool.

Different rules apply to different roles. Students know that they are students – not professors. They take their seats in the lecture hall at the appointed time and do not stand front and centre at the podium.

When the rules are vague or conflicting, or when people are unsure about which role they are supposed to play, decision-making becomes more difficult. Should they intervene or call the police when they witness a fistfight? How should they behave when they are unsure if a person lying on the pavement is alive or dead?

Whose job is it to pick up litter from the street? It can be hard to reconcile conflicting rules. The traffic rules say that a cyclist is not allowed to cross an intersection against a red light, but the cyclist is also a mother in a hurry who wants to follow the preschool's rules on collection times.

A Repertoire of Identities

People's decisions shift with the situation and the roles they play in different situations. They find it natural to use a repertoire of identities, which presume discrete rule systems and may result in radically different behaviours (Veyne 1983). People adapt their behaviour to situations and roles so dramatically that not much seems to be left of the stable core that is assumed to constitute individuality. But if people manage to separate the various situations in their minds, they need not perceive any conflict among roles. They can maintain the belief that they constitute *one* individual; they may change their minds now and then, but still remain 'the same old me'.

Author Leif Zern (2012) provides an example of the separation of various identities in a story about his father, who followed Jewish laws and rituals. But his father was also a modern Swede with a summer cottage. Despite the Jewish prohibition against eating shellfish, the family regularly arranged crayfish parties at their summer cottage. But their Jewish relatives were never invited. Zern argues that his father was able to live in two worlds – his country life and his city life – without conflict.

People can follow rules when they know who they are – when they can answer the question: *What kind of person am I?* But they can also acquire an identity by deciding to follow the rules that a person with a particular kind of identity is expected to follow. In this case, the rule following comes first, followed by the identity, rather than the opposite. People demonstrate that they belong to the cadre of friends of the environment by deciding to follow the rules of behaviour established by environmental organizations: for example, choosing eco-friendly travel (or no travel at all), lowering the temperature indoors or buying organic food. In sports, one can obtain a high-status identity by jumping high, provided that one follows the rules that apply to the high jump.

The Sentimentalist Fallacy

Separating situations and keeping them apart is obviously easier when they are perceived as intrinsically different. Philosopher William James ([1906]2012, p. 96) wrote about the 'sentimentalist fallacy' committed when people admire principles that they ignore in practice. In *Swann's Way*, the first volume of *In Search of Lost Time* (Proust [1913]2003), the maid, Francoise, is able to lament over calamities that occurred on the other side of the planet, while behaving harshly towards her daughter and son-in-law.

Principles are similar to distance in this respect. Many people are in favour of using public transportation, buying Fair Trade groceries and donating blood, yet believe that they are prevented from acting according to their principles at the moment. *Right now*, they must behave as they usually do. They are prepared to make a new decision, but not now. Later.

Framing

The decisions people make depend upon their understanding of an issue or a problem with which they are confronted: the *framing* of the problem. Kahneman (2011, p. 371) tells the story of two women who encounter difficulties when they are on the way to see a play:

> A woman has bought two $80 tickets to the theatre. When she arrives at the theatre, she opens her wallet and discovers that the tickets are missing. Will she buy two more tickets to see the play?

> A woman goes to the theatre, intending to buy two tickets that cost $80 each. She arrives at the theatre, opens her wallet, and discovers to her dismay that the $160 with which she was going to make the purchase is missing. She could use her credit card. Will she buy the tickets?

Respondents argued differently depending on how the question was framed. Respondents who believed that the woman who lost her tickets were more likely to say that she would go home without seeing the play, whereas respondents who were told that the woman lost the money she had set aside said that she would probably buy the tickets with her credit card. In both cases, the $160 is money lost forever – a *sunk cost*. People who make rational decisions based on the logic of consequences should not care about sunk costs, because they refer to circumstances beyond their influence. What's gone is gone.

But many of the people who were asked to determine if the women will see the play argue that tickets differ from money. The woman who has lost the tickets may as well go home. But for the woman who lost her money, money is money; certainly she will be poorer than she would have been when she is forced to buy replacement tickets, but this is a loss she is likely willing to accept. The different ways of thinking are attributed to different situations with different rules, and people do not necessarily realize that their judgement depends on the framing of the question.

Similarly, people treat chances and risks differently. If the situation involves the chance of a prize, they tend to choose the certain over the uncertain and prefer a smaller but certain prize to a bigger prize if there is some, albeit small, probability that they will win nothing. If the matter involves losses, however, they reason in the opposite way. They are likely to risk a large loss rather than certainly incurring a more limited one (Tversky and Kahneman 1986). This behaviour can be described as inconsistent and is usually presented that way. But it may just as well be interpreted to mean that people have a tendency to follow different rules in different situations. The effect is that an option that seemed at one time to be the best by far can be reframed so it becomes equally obvious to decision makers that it is no longer attractive.

IMITATION AND EXPERIMENTATION

Imitation and experimentation are elements of upbringing and education: Children and adolescents learn by imitating parents, friends and idols. Adults are likely to imitate those they consider to be in their same category: in clothing style, eating habits and home décor; in the clubs or organizations they join or resign from; and what they name their children. In addition, they imitate themselves – by remembering what they have done in a similar situation in the past. In this way, imitation helps maintain identity. Like the logic of appropriateness, imitation may also be an attempt at creating a new identity. To become a hip-hopper, one imitates the hairstyle and music taste of hip-hoppers.

Experimentation is another way of creating identity. Author Thomas Mann (who understood decisiveness to be a masculine trait) described how young men are given an opportunity to develop their identity when they test 'one possible view out of many hovering in the air' (*eine der möglichen und in der Luft schwebenden Anschauungen*, Mann [1924]1974, p. 139).

Experimentation is used in less grandiose contexts as well. It serves to simplify decision-making, rendering it less uncertain and helping decision makers learn for the future. Using experimentation, people make preliminary decisions, which they know they can back out of if they do not like the outcome. They buy a jacket, knowing that they can return it within a certain number of days; they move in with someone they love, but do not get married; they buy train tickets that can be exchanged. Decisions that people know from the outset will remain valid only for a short while work like an experiment: a trial subscription to a newspaper; a 'have-a-go' card at the gym; or a date with someone they met online.

At best, experiments provide people with insights into their own preferences, allowing them to learn *who they are* in various situations. Like Mann's young men, they become better acquainted with their preferences, while simultaneously gaining a better understanding of the implications of their decision and whether they like it or not. This understanding is better founded than the imaginary scenarios that serve as the basis of following the logic of consequences. Experimentation may help to clear up the decision situation, because decision makers have the opportunity to change their position without serious loss of face. They can even abandon projects they have set in motion. It is easier for them to determine which further decisions they will make – if any decisions are necessary.

There is obviously the risk that imitation or experimentation fail and that the decision makers learn the wrong things (March and Olsen 1975). Perhaps they misunderstand a situation and base their decisions on this misunderstanding – until they have made several decisions and eventually discover their error. (And should it turn out that they never discover they have drawn the wrong conclusions from their past decisions, perhaps no harm was done.)

Intuition and Emotions

Intuition (often called 'gut feelings') tends to be laden with romantic overtones – like a notion of the subconscious as something mystical, magical, beyond intelligence and logics. This interpretation enjoys little support in psychological research, however (Simon 1987). Instead, intuition is a way for people to use their cumulative experience. It becomes synonymous with 'tacit knowledge' – the experience people have acquired by having been in similar decision situations in the past. People who use their intuition collect their information not from others, but from their own memory. They use their experience to understand which decision they should make.

Experience and intuition are often confounded in chess. The general presumption is that skilled chess players should be analytical and systematic – and slow. But professional chess players have the capacity to play many games simultaneously – and fast. It seems reasonable to assume that professional judgement in other areas of life similarly develop with time (Simon 1987).

The same argument applies to people in crisis: They re-use old information gathered in situations that they perceive as similar to the current one. Intuition then becomes a type of logic of appropriateness or a matter of decision makers imitating themselves. In the best case, they get so good at it that they are able to understand more complex connections than they would if they had gone through an elaborate decision process.

In a novel decision situation, however, experience-based intuition may lead decision makers down the garden path. They misjudge the new situation and fail to notice that it differs from situations they have experienced. They draw conclusions that worked in the past but no longer do. This situation occurs in disasters, when it becomes necessary to depart from procedures that work well under normal circumstances. In these cases, people have a tendency – despite everything and to the bitter end – to use their experience to behave as they usually do (Weick 1996, 2007). This is what happened to the Swedish government administration at the time of the tsunami in 2004. (See the end of the book.)

At worst, people do not notice that their previous decisions were based on false assumptions. They imitate their own false conclusions and make the wrong decision again and again. Without investigating the matter further, they perceive the familiar circumstances – the circumstances that someone in authority tells them about or circumstances they have heard repeated as truth. They become inclined to believe some Facebook rumour or urban legend – like the story of the rats in the pizza.

The term 'intuition' is also used to describe how decision makers acquire information in a decision process. In many situations, according to this definition, people use their experience (including their biases) in what appears to be intuitively when they are introduced to and instantly evaluate a stranger. They categorize others by gender, height, age, hair colour and hairstyle; judge their sense of fashion; notice their dialect; guess their occupation; and quickly determine how they should relate to them. They are often relatively correct in their assessments – at least in their own minds – and this has been borne out by research. In one experiment, students were shown videos of various teachers in action for a couple of seconds. They assessed these teachers in approximately the same way as did students who had been taught by these teachers for an entire semester (Gladwell 2005).

The more relevant information people have, the better their chances of making intuitive decisions that turn out to be 'good' or 'right'. In some situations, they learn to differentiate information quickly, discarding the unimportant and using the important. They can get so good at it that it seems as if they are acting by reflex, without making any decision.

The consequences of intuitive decisions are twofold, then: Either people make decisions they are satisfied with in a quick and inexpensive way, without having to spend precious time gathering more information. Or intuition leads them astray: to misguided conclusions and positions. In both cases, intuition resembles rule following and imitation. The decision makers build on their past behaviour and refer retrospectively rather than prospectively, as required by the logic of consequences and the model of rational decision-making.

This reference to experience or perceptions becomes even more apparent when decision makers make decisions based on what they *feel* is right. Emotions are – perhaps – more intuitive than intuition. (And perhaps, in a so-called post-truth society, they come to play a more prominent role.)

Philosopher David Hume ([1772]2004) argued that value judgements are based on emotions. Do people who rely on their intuition
actually proceed from how they *feel* when facing a decision? Are
emotions the same thing as cumulative experience, or something
fundamentally different? Could it be that the emotions – the origins
of which are unknown – come first, and are followed by particular
preferences and experiences?

Pizzorno (1990, cited in Boltanski and Thévenot [1991]2006)
argued that people vote for a political party because they *feel* that
the party fits them, giving no thought to how this choice would
benefit them, even though they may later base their arguments on
those premises. Affect or fleeting moods obviously influence
people's judgements and the decisions they make. Insecure or timid
individuals are cautious and concerned about the basis for their
decisions. Angry individuals tend to be optimistic. Like happy
people, they are inclined to rely on simple rules of thumb that they
believe have worked in the past (Schwartz 2000). People who are
stressed, on the other hand, tend to ignore their expert knowledge
and rely on their emotions – perhaps because they must make a
firm decision before a specified time or because they realize they
must make an unpleasant decision (Finucane et al. 2000; Simon
1987). Their feelings work as a sort of distillation of more general
experience, which is not adapted to a particular judgement or
decision situation. Consequently, people who have a positive attitude towards smoking, alcohol or food additives tend to under-
estimate the risks of smoking, drinking alcohol, or eating food with
chemical additives. In contrast, those who dislike these phenomena
judge the risks to be considerably higher (Finucane et al. 2000).

REGRETS

As shown, the notion that decision makers have the option to
choose something else is intrinsic to the very concept of decision.
By definition, decision makers take the risk of making the wrong
choice – a choice that they come to regret.

All human beings – except perhaps the very youngest – have
regretted something, sometime. The feeling that they should have
acted differently relates to the optimism of many decisive individuals. If it is more the rule than the exception that decision

makers tend to over-estimate the positive effects of their decisions, it is also normal that they feel disappointed in retrospect (Harrison and March 1984). Research demonstrates that people tend to judge themselves harshly. They imagine after the fact that they knew more than they actually did know when the decision was made (Fischhoff 1975). When they know (or believe they know) the outcome of various events, they see connections and courses of events that they believe they should also have been able to judge in advance.

People who regret their decisions believe that they could have postponed the decision or made a different decision. Later they imagine that they would have made a better decision if only they had given themselves time to think. They should have realized what they actually wanted to achieve, found out the right rule, or investigated how others had decided in similar situations. Or they could have experimented by making decisions about one thing at a time. For those using the logic of consequences, Benjamin Franklin's moral algebra does not seem as risible post-decision as it seemed pre-decision.

In particular, people who acted impulsively may regret their impulsiveness and lack of reflection. If they had considered a decision more carefully in advance, they would have been able to imagine that they might regret the decision. Reflection could have acted as a warning signal from the outset when they made their decision (Simonson 1989). Now they find it embarrassing and awkward that they did not figure out what is really important to them until it was too late. They fear that others will draw conclusions about the kind of people they are dealing with – and even feel *schadenfreude* – when they observe the unfortunate decision.

Some people envision future regrets even before they have made a decision. Others use threats of regret to caution against decisions about to be made: 'If you do that, you are sure to regret it.' This type of decision maker (or their friends and loved ones) then use imaginary regrets as arguments in favour of further reflection – and in favour of the logic of consequences. According to this line of reasoning, regret should already be considered a possible consequence when a decision is made. Post-decision disappointment then becomes an integral part of the decision-making process.

People seem to be less regretful when they base their decisions on the recommendations of an expert, probably because they then have someone to blame. It becomes another, less risky way to make decisions and may not be perceived as decision-making at all (Kahneman 2011).

Excuses

Given the unpleasant feeling generated by regret, it is no surprise that people resort to various arguments to avoid it. At the very least, they do not want to have to tell everybody and his brother that they regret their actions.

Decision makers use the phrase 'in hindsight' to show that, despite everything, they did their best. Those who use this expression are not saying they regret what they have done; rather they are finding reasons to shift the blame. They denote that although it is *now* fairly easy to figure out how a particular decision should have been designed, a great deal of valuable information was impossible to obtain when the decision was made.

Failures may also be more directly blamed on people or circumstances unrelated to the decision maker. People commonly describe themselves – if possible – as victims of circumstances for which someone else is responsible; they tend to disclaim responsibility for poor outcomes. It seems equally common – still, if within reason – to claim involvement in decisions that are subsequently considered successful (Langer 1975; Beckman 1990). Excuses serve to atone for decisions that are found lacking, but they become superfluous when – as it turns out – other people like those decisions.

As noted, people who reason according to the logic of consequences may change their preferences while in the process of deciding. After a decision is made, and its consequences become apparent, they have another opportunity to change their preferences and lower their ambitions. Given that things turned out as they did, they persuade themselves and others that things turned out pretty well after all. Optimism and high ambitions were necessary when the decision was made; otherwise there might not have been any decision at all. But in retrospect, a more realistic attitude and lower ambitions are justified (Harrison and March 1984).

Through post-hoc rationalization, people reconstruct their decision-making in line with the logic of consequences – whether consciously or unconsciously. Similarly, they reshape and adjust their evaluation of the outcomes of their decisions. They adapt to others' expectations and construct a context for their decisions in which they have eliminated the embarrassing elements that they did not wish to acknowledge.

RATIONALITY AS A RULE

Scholars are remarkably fond of describing people's choices and decisions in terms of rationality. Even the numerous organizational scholars, psychologists and social psychologists who persuasively show that it is unrealistic to expect people to follow the rules of rationality proceed from these rules when they construct a different kind of rationality – which they tag as closer to reality, yet still as rationality. These scholars use the model of rational decision-making as an obvious reference, which they describe as 'traditional', 'typical', even 'classic'. How people generally reason and make decisions becomes an anomaly in need of definition. Scholars talk about *approximate* rationality, *ecological* rationality, *social* rationality, *situational* rationality, *process* rationality, *flexible* rationality, *selective* rationality and *retrospective* rationality – even *romantic* rationality (Gigerenzer and Todd 1999; Habermas [1981]1984; March 1978; Perrow 1986; Simon 1955). But when many different conditions are categorized under the term 'rationality', the concept loses its pertinent meaning.

Perhaps there is something irresistible in the notion that people can really see into the future. Perhaps it does not matter that this notion is admittedly unrealistic; perhaps that even adds to its appeal. In this way, rationality takes on both moral and aesthetic overtones – its clear and universally applicable tenets seem right, even beautiful.

Scholars who describe how people actually behave when they make decisions also have a normative – and educative – message in favour of rationality (Shapira 2008). Social psychologists even want people to do the 'right' thing. They encourage influential decision makers to exploit knowledge about the way individuals make decisions. Because they know that people are affected by the way a choice situation is presented (the framing of the situation), they seek to influence behaviour by designing decision situations in a specific way. Many people will then choose the options that the scholars prefer, but without necessarily understanding this to be the case. Thaler and Sunstein (2008), for example, recommend that sausage should be labelled 'contains 10% fat' rather than '90% fat-free' – because people will then eat less sausage. Similarly, people are persuaded to save for their pensions by promising that *next time* they get a pay increase, they will set aside money for their pension, because it is easier for them to comply with principles that do not affect them immediately. The method is the same as that used by marketers, although their idea is to satisfy the interests of a particular organization by persuading people to go ahead and buy that sausage, irrespective of its fat content.

3. Organizations as decision makers

Decisions are fundamental to organizations: Organizations were founded as a result of a decision, and they continue to make decisions about what they shall do and how. Some members of organizations make decisions about the way other members shall act. Organizations have been defined as consisting of decisions only (Luhmann 2000) or as 'decided orders' (Ahrne and Brunsson 2011).

Organizations are not physical entities like individuals, but social constructions with individuals as their model. It is impossible to *see* organizations. In order to convince people that an organization exists, it must be represented in rough accordance with generally accepted presumptions of what constitutes an organization. Organizations are frequently treated as *legal persons*. Just like individuals, they make statements about one issue or another.

'Sandvik plans to invest in …'
'The authority has no means of …'

Organizations can even be emotional:

'The Government regards with apprehension the proposal that …'
'The social security board is delighted to find …'

Not least, organizations make decisions! And they frequently make a point of publishing the most significant ones. A closer look reveals, however, that one or more individuals made the decision on the organization's behalf. Whether there is any significant difference between individual and organizational decision-making, then, becomes a relevant question. One would expect people to behave in roughly the same way, regardless of whether they are making decisions on their own behalf or on behalf of an organization.

Organizational scholars like Herbert Simon observed no critical differences between individual and organizational decision-making. Simon considered bounded rationality a natural consequence of the

Decisions

difficulties everyone encounters in making rational decisions
(Simon 1955; see Chapter 2).

Others say that it is certainly reasonable to imagine that people
make judgements in about the same way, regardless of whether they
are part of an organization or not, but argue that decision-making in
organizations differs from individual decision-making. Many studies of individual decision-making were conducted as experiments in
a laboratory setting, and often with students as participants. So
individual decision-making was studied under circumstances that
rarely if ever apply in practice – neither for individuals nor for
organizations. (See Table 3.1.)

Table 3.1 Individual and organizational decision-making

The following applies to experiments on individuals	But the following applies to organizations in practice
Subjects are presented with clear information as a basis for their decisions	The information available to decision makers is often ambiguous
The activity is expected to be limited in time	The organization should survive for the foreseeable future
The 'decisions' are unique and will not be repeated	Similar decisions have been actualized and will be actualized repeatedly
The decisions have no significant effects	The decisions have tangible effects on decision makers and their organizations
Only individual decision makers are involved	Decision makers are involved in a social context, where people have different opinions and risk discord, where some people are particularly dominant and where incentives and penalties are used to influence the behaviour of members of the organization

Source: After Shapira (2008).

Organizational decisions affect more people than the decision
makers, and they usually affect them in a more radical way than do
decisions made by individuals. When organizations make decisions,
both members of the organization and outsiders are affected. As
organizational decision makers, people usually have considerably
greater resources available than they do as private individuals. And

they have the right to try to force organization members to comply with their decisions – although they do not always succeed.

But organizational decision makers cannot make any decisions: They should be loyal to their organization and design their decision-making not with reference to their private preferences, but by their assessment of what will be the best outcome for the organization (Barnard [1938]1968; Fayol [1916]1949), despite the obvious difficulties of always making this distinction.

Another constraint concerns the fact that several decision makers may be involved in a given decision, are expected to make it jointly, and must come to an agreement (Haug 2015). Those who are keen to ensure that the decision genuinely affects the organization's actions – and does not remain a mere decision – need to ascertain in advance that the decision will be accepted by those who should implement it.

These observations imply that it makes sense to treat organizational decisions as a separate decision category. There are many decision makers to keep track of in large organizations, and *who* makes which decisions becomes a critical question. Because organizations are supposed to achieve change and often perceive their environments to be rapidly changing, even turbulent, *when* decisions are made is also critical. The question of *how* decisions are made is as relevant to organizations as it is to individuals, but this question is complicated by the existence of numerous decision makers and by the fact that many decisions affect a large number of individuals or other organizations. In this chapter, we discuss these questions in this order: who, when and how.

WHO MAKES DECISIONS IN ORGANIZATIONS?

Organizational decision-making is so important that there are decision-making rules in the form of constitutions that specify who shall make decisions. The constitution may require all members of the organization to make joint decisions in certain situations, such as by referendum. But more commonly, there are rules for the decisions that various organizational members are allowed to make.

Some members of the organization may be allowed to make decisions that apply to all activities of the organization, whereas the decision-making powers of others are confined to specific parts of these activities, and many organization members are allowed to make few, if any, decisions on behalf of the organization. Some members are allowed to decide on large expenditures, others can decide only on small expenditures. Some are allowed to decide who shall belong to the organization at any given time and what these people shall do.

A decision by managers at the top of the organizational hierarchy usually leads to many more decisions further down in the hierarchy; and through this process, a great many people become decision makers. Decisions that directly affect the activities of the organization are at least as critical to the organization's success as are the so-called strategic, long-term decisions formulated in general terms and made by top managers or top politicians.

In large organizations, some members become specialists on specific decisions, such as investments or the enrolling of new members, and their decisions can affect other parts of the organization, even its external reputation. Human resource specialists, for example, are often allowed to hire – to decide whether another individual should belong to the organization. Even though the new recruit may initially be paid a low wage, these specialists are making a major future expenditure decision on behalf of their organization. For it is possible that the individual will stay with the organization for many years – for better or for worse.

WHEN ARE DECISIONS MADE?

Decision makers in organizations are expected to report their decisions to their colleagues, and often to outsiders as well. At the same time, they describe the future actions they have planned. They are also expected to justify their decisions, but it is by no means certain that they will successfully persuade others of the wisdom of the decisions. Rather, their decisions may lead to criticism and active attempts to block the decided actions. For this reason, decision makers may be tempted to avoid decisions and seek strategies for getting their way in other, less tangible ways – working behind the scenes. People who want to understand how power is exerted in organizations cannot settle for studying decisions and their effects. They must also study situations in which decisions were *not* made (Bachrach and Baratz 1970).

People who want to challenge the powers of appointed decision makers have an interest in forcing a decision, so it is clear what and whom they oppose – and this before any controversial actions have been taken. It is a central principle of democracy that decisions shall precede important organizational actions, making it clear who the decision makers are and forcing them to justify their positions and discuss those decisions with others.

Avoiding decisions is not only a strategy for gaining power, but also a mundane matter of saving time and effort. Difficult issues may resolve themselves without any decisions, if only one is patient and does not act hastily. When decisions are piled together, they may 'rot from the bottom up', and matters initiated long ago that are no longer topical can be stricken from the agenda without any decision maker ever having to take a position on the issue.

But decision makers also need to find the right time to make their decisions. Decisions can be made too early, so that they have to be corrected later when things turn out differently. Or they can be made too late, so that they cannot stop a development that has already started.

Decision makers cannot always control the timing of their decision-making. Others may require a decision before the decision makers are ready to make one. In other cases, decision makers are unable to make a decision because they perceive the situation to be so murky that they simply do not know what to decide. They are caught in a maelstrom of changes that are beyond their control and which are affecting their organization in unpredictable ways, both positively and negatively. Even if they think that they understand what is happening, they are unable to find a way out.

Organizational decision makers, like any individual decision maker, have limited capacity to observe all problems and opportunities that should be the object for decisions. They make decisions in areas that they happen to attend to, and decisions in other areas are dependent upon their redirecting their attention (Cyert and March [1963]1992). What decision makers attend to may be the result of events that are conspicuous, but not crucial for the organization (Tengblad 2000).

Unexpected events may shift the attention of decision makers to yet further new issues. A matter that seemed urgent at one time is forgotten, and after a while is no longer up for decision-making. Nor do organizations necessarily need to solve every problem that somebody finds irritating. Wealthy organizations may live with quite a few unresolved problems that they imagine they will deal with later or hope will be forgotten or eventually dissipate.

The ability of decision makers to notice various options is critical – so critical that this ability, in particular, determines if an organization succeeds or fails (Denrell 2012; Ocasio 1997). How decision makers understand and formulate the need for change determines which decisions they make. Options that no one notices will not be considered; they do not exist for the moment.

In conclusion, decision-making takes on a certain air of randomness. It is no longer an issue of the systematic work required by the model of rational decision-making. Rather, the decisions will be conditional upon the problems and opportunities that decision makers happen to observe and how they define and delimit their possibilities to make – or avoid – particular decisions.

The ability of decision makers to notice discrete issues, their interest in doing so, pressures from external stakeholders, and pure coincidence, all determine when decisions are made and what they imply. Decision makers can be more or less insightful in understanding the importance of timing and more or less skilled at taking advantage of those times.

According to a somewhat extended version of the model of rational decision-making, problems generate a need for decision-making by people responsible for the relevant area – people who start searching for options that would solve the problem and choose the option with the best consequences. But assuming that flows of problems, options, decision makers, and decision opportunities are relatively independent of each other, decision-making processes become less orderly and more dependent on time than on logic. They can, in fact, be described by a 'garbage can model of organizational choice' (Cohen et al. 1972).

According to this model, an organization constantly meets new problems and options. There are several people with decision-making authority more or less interested in or attending to certain problems and options. In addition, there are a limited number of opportunities for making decisions – only a limited number of meetings in which decisions can be made or a limited number of events urging anybody to ask for a decision to be made. Which decision makers show up at a meeting influences the problems and solutions that are discussed. Decision makers' preferences change over time, when, for example, they consider aspects of an option they had previously ignored, or when a third option arrives and distracts them, changing their priorities (Denrell 2012). Furthermore, the problems and solutions that decision makers attend to vary over time, depending on factors outside their control. Sometimes a problem can be fitted to a decision maker's favourite solution, or a solution is found that fits a favourite problem, making a decision on that solution more likely. To use the Cohen et al. (1972) formulations, the organization

> is a collection of choices looking for problems, issues and feelings looking for decision situations in which they might be aired, solutions looking for issues to which they might be the answer, and decision makers looking for work. (Cohen et al. 1972, p. 2)

And a decision opportunity is

> a garbage can into which various kinds of problems and solutions are dumped by participants as they are generated. The mix of garbage in a single can depends on the mix of cans available, on the labels attached to the alternative cans, on what garbage is currently produced, and on the speed with which garbage is collected and removed from the scene. (Cohen et al. 1972, p. 2)

In other words, the decisions made by the organization depend on the constellation of problems, solutions (options), and participants who happen to be present at each decision-making opportunity. This constellation varies over time, and the timing of decision opportunities becomes a key factor for the outcome. The exact combination of these influxes influences the likelihood that problems or options will be eliminated. If not, they persist, waiting, perhaps for some future decision-making opportunity.

The garbage can model was originally developed after studies of organizations with vague goals, fuzzy connections between activities and goal attainment, and fluid participation in decision-making – organizations such as universities. More recently, it has been argued that the model aptly describes vital aspects of virtually any organization, although it must be modified in consideration of the established decision procedures in many organizations (Levinthal 2012; Ocasio 2012). When there is a decision procedure with rules stipulating that specific decisions must be made at specific times, the issue to be handled is a given, as are many of the options decision makers must consider. There is often room for randomness, however, even within the framework of established decision procedures. Procedures rarely govern everything and are rarely followed to the last detail (Musselin 1996).

HOW DO ORGANIZATIONS MAKE DECISIONS?

Scholars and organizational consultants usually emphasize the importance of making the *right* decision. Bad decisions have an adverse impact on both the organization and its decision makers, as Hammond, Keeney and Raiffa (1998, p. 47) have noted:

> Making decisions is the most important job of any executive. It's also the toughest and the riskiest. Bad decisions can damage a business and a career, sometimes irreparably. So where do bad decisions come from?

Like social psychologists, these scholars and consultants aim to school the decision makers. People need to get better at making decisions, both as individuals and as organizational decision makers, they contend. Organizational decision makers, in particular, must avoid illogical and emotional thinking. They must not give credence to irrelevant circumstances, such as their gut feelings. They should clarify what they want to achieve and use their goals to choose among discrete options. In short, they should make every possible attempt to apply the model of rational decision-making.

This normative approach is based on oversimplified presumptions, however, because decision makers in organizations are frequently caught up in an *omnium-gatherum* of trends, events, opinions and pressures. Even when they do base their decisions on assessments of the future, therefore, their logic-of-consequences reasoning takes on a different – more realistic and human – character than it does when expressed in the rules of the model of rational decision-making.

What is Going On?

Not only must decision makers in organizations make decisions that promote the success of their organizations, they must do it jointly with others – others who often have different roles, divergent opinions and different interpretations of what is happening – people who draw different conclusions. Nor can any member of large organizations with complex operations have knowledge of all the activities being pursued by their organization (Fayol [1916]1949; Stein 1999).

The notion that the world has never before changed at such a fast pace as it is changing now is probably an exaggeration, but the environments of many organizations are changing in ways that are difficult to predict. This is true even when the changes are due to actions initiated by the organization itself. In addition, internal change is a characteristic feature of all organizations: Colleagues leave and new colleagues are recruited, operations are restructured, new technologies are introduced and new rules for the organization are established.

Before they make any decisions, decision makers in organizations need to ask themselves: *What is actually going on?* They need to create a context that they consider reasonable and that they can put into words and communicate to others (Weick et al. 2005).

There is a need for *sense making*: making sense of a situation and successfully recounting it to others. Sense making involves learning – or imagining – not only what has happened, but also what may happen. Decision makers who try to impose order on a decision situation first create an understanding of the organization's development. Organizational accounts – the annual report, press releases, interviews with the top officials – play a key role in creating a view of what happened and what is the present situation that many people find convincing and share. In this way, accounts help improve the conditions for making decisions that will be widely accepted.

One way of experimenting with future decisions is to design *strategies* – a pursuit that large organizations in particular tend to undertake. Through their strategies, organizations communicate the type of organization they are and want to be – the identity that they want others to share. Through these strategies, they express long-term goals; at times they also express what they are going to devote special attention to in the near or relatively distant future. Many strategies are written in such general terms that they seem equally applicable to different organizations and different types of organizations: They seem to provide little guidance for particular decisions, but justify several different types of decisions. Their imprecise formulation makes sense because of the unclear relationship between organizational activities and organizational success; many future decisions may prove equally valuable to the organization (Levinthal 2012). But despite their general, imprecise formulations, strategies are usually placed in the category of 'important' decisions. They give organizational members the opportunity to sense how external stakeholders perceive them. Strategies may also be used to justify decisions (or the lack of decision-making) or as arguments in post-hoc rationalization. Again, an imprecise strategy becomes advantageous.

Before they make a critical decision, experienced, sense-making decision makers feel their way forward by discussing their conclusions with others inside and outside the organization. In this way, they determine if they have perceived the situation in about the same way as others do, and they gain the opportunity to persuade others that the decision is reasonable prior to making the decision. They *garner support* for the decision. If it turns out that the decision makers have a radically different understanding of the situation and what needs to be done, they have the opportunity to change their minds. Or perhaps they are convinced they are right, but in the process they learn the arguments they are going to need to justify a decision that they realize many people are going to question.

Decision makers' sense making of their decision situation need not necessarily be accurate in any objective sense. Even for decision makers who have erred in their decision, it can be important to *believe* that they understand the situation they are intervening in through their decision. Like the Hungarian soldiers who survived in the Alps by using a map of the Pyrenees, decision makers need to trust the information they are using. (Remember that St. Peter fell in the water when he lost faith.)

Studies show that decision makers in organizations get things wrong to a surprisingly large extent and in many ways (Mezias and Starbuck 2003). They make the same mistakes as they do when making decisions in their personal lives – ascribing unwarranted importance to recent and dramatic events, for instance. Or they may have a difficult time changing a decision once it is made, even though they believe it to be wrong (Staw and Ross 1987). In organizations, their mistakes may be compounded by the failure to notice their missteps. Perhaps they are surrounded by sycophants who pass on the information they believe decision makers want to hear, or perhaps the decision makers themselves are located too far from the activities where their decisions are to be implemented.

Information systems, which exist to make it easier for decision makers to interpret events in their organization and its environment may lead to misunderstandings and fallacious interpretations when the decision makers do not understand the information they are given. Such systems may encourage decision makers to follow old habits when gathering information, so they fail to pick up new trends or unexpected developments.

Yet decisions made on fallacious grounds are not necessarily bad decisions. If decision makers have access to a basis for their decision-making that seems logical and reasonable, chances are that their decision will be generally accepted, a circumstance that aligns well with what is usually called 'accepted opinion'.

It may therefore suffice that the decision makers refer to information that others find relevant and trustworthy. When the goal of the decision maker is to get something done – and that is usually important in organizations – it may be more important that decisions be made than that the decision makers have access to perfect decision input. The decision makers' conviction that they are right – and their perseverance when it comes to convincing others that they are – may be more important than their analytical skill (Porac and Rosa 1996; Swieringa and Weick 1987).

The Art of Consensus

There are antagonisms in many contexts in which people come together with a view to reaching agreement, and new antagonisms arise once these discussions are underway. This applies not least when people are expected to achieve something together – as in organizations. There are numerous ways of reaching consensus, however.

Sometimes discussions lead to some parties *convincing* others that their mode of reasoning is the right one. They have arguments that the others were unaware of. Or they exploit their authority as experts in a field. In other cases, one or more people *persuade* others to go along with their proposals for the design of a decision. They argue that the decision is not important enough for the other party to object. Or they make it seem likely that the relationship between the parties will deteriorate should the opposition persist.

Decision makers can also *negotiate* with their colleagues before they make final decisions. Negotiations regularly precede decisions on budgets, salaries, major organizational changes or other changes that affect the members of an organization. In the ideal situation, negotiations lead to novel thinking; the negotiating parties learn from each other and arrive jointly at solutions that had not previously occurred to any one individual (Follett 1941). Less ideally, the parties engaged in negotiations foresee that they will be forced to compromise, and they start by exaggerating their demands and expectations, leaving a little wiggle room in their proposed decision. The leeway cannot be too large, however; if it is, they may be perceived as frivolous, and the entire negotiation may come to a standstill (Wildavsky 1975).

When a negotiation results in *compromises*, in fact, the participants usually express dissatisfaction with the outcome, while simultaneously claiming that they have acted responsibly and realistically. Without their willingness to compromise, they assert, no decision would have been made. Budget and salary negotiations are routinely described in this manner – simultaneously described as unsatisfactory and successful (Due and Madsen 1996). Should any participants find in their heart of hearts that they did not really need to compromise, but were granted their demands, they would rarely be willing to admit it, as this would put them in an inferior position in a later round of negotiations. Next year somebody might remember how successful they were the previous year and demand especially harsh treatment (Holmblad Brunsson 2013).

Barter transactions are a special type of compromise in which one party goes along with the other party's proposal, provided that a proposal by the first party is met. Then one party is satisfied with one proposal but dissatisfied with the other, while the relationship is the opposite for the other party. The various proposals need not have much to do with each other, but may refer to problems that concern different parts of the organization's activities and even entail promises about future decisions (Brunsson et al. 1990). The local union branch accepts the outsourcing of payroll administration in exchange for the employer paying for fitness and wellness programmes during working hours. Or the government accepts a more generous policy for accepting refugees in exchange for the opposition agreeing to an increase in military spending.

Yet another way of reaching consensus is by *expressing the content of the decision vaguely*, so that all parties can embrace it (Sahlin-Andersson 1989). The decision makers then leave it up to others to interpret – and agree upon! – whatever is actually meant. Current conflicts are obscured, but may crystallize again once the decisions are to be implemented.

Antagonisms arise when people know what they want. They are familiar with their own preferences and want the opportunity to at least voice their dissenting opinion before a decision is made. But there are many issues for which people have a lack of commitment one way or another. Although they are designated decision makers, expected to participate in a decision on the same terms as others, in practice they leave it up to others to decide. Consequently, a group of decision makers is able to reach consensus merely because some members of the group do not actively oppose the decision – which does not mean that they necessarily consider it a good decision (Haug 2015).

Irrationality

Several examples of irrationality in organizations are consistent with or add to those found in individual decision-making. As Cyert and March ([1963]1992) argued, decision makers handle the fact that they have several goals by considering one goal at a time rather than letting their decisions be guided by a preference function, by which each goal is weighed according to its importance. Furthermore, they adapt their preferences to the option they are discussing rather than the other way round, so that that option seems much more positive or much more negative than it would if more preferences had been evoked. Even organizations with extensive resources for investigation tend to be frugal in seeking the options they consider. There are decision processes in which only one alternative is considered, and when two options are considered, one is used as an inferior contrast to the superior one. Even when more options are investigated, the search is often limited to those that are close to the present situation (Lindblom 1959; Cyert and March [1963]1992). And the search is terminated when a satisfactory option is found, thus missing the chance of finding the optimal one (Simon 1955). The satisfactory option depends on the decision maker's level of aspiration, but that level is adapted to the options of which the decision maker is aware, a circumstance that further reduces the search for options.

THREE EXAMPLES

In this section, we provide three examples of how decision situations evolve in ways that undermine the feasibility of rational decision-making.

1. Calculation, which is designed as a rational method for preparing a decision, may evolve into support for decisions that decision makers have already decided upon.
2. Collective decision-making, which could involve a thorough investigation of various decision options, may evolve into monocultures, in which decision makers are virtually incapable of considering information that conflicts with their preconceptions.
3. Obvious failures, which should induce decision makers to think again, may, on the contrary, induce them to make further bad decisions.

Calculation

A *calculation* is an estimation of what is going to happen, given certain goals and assumptions. It reflects the logic of consequences. Ideally, the predicted consequences are expressed in a single unit of measurement, such as money. A single unit of measurement makes it easier to compare options; they can be ordered on a single scale from good to bad, from most profitable to least profitable, and so on. Such a scale makes it easier to make decisions according to the rules of rationality – or so it may seem. The problem becomes that of converting various types of consequences into the same unit of measurement. Can you compare apples and oranges? Money now with money in the future? The value of extinct flora and fauna with the value of economic growth for people who are currently living in poverty? Should decision makers have the type of preferences that makes possible a conversion into one single measurement, a calculation can guide their decision. When that is not the case, the calculation, however concise and elegant, becomes irrelevant.

Yet, decision makers who say that they have based their decision on a calculation seem to have good reasons for their decision, not least because they appear to have applied the model of rational decision-making. The results of a calculation that are presented in aggregate form become clear and comprehensible. In the best case, the decision makers can compare different options in economic terms. On the other hand, a perfect calculation that matches the preferences of the decision maker means that decision makers become superfluous; those who prepared the calculation have already figured out what the decision should be.

Some people allow themselves to be impressed by calculations; others see them as a reason to scrutinize both the fundamental premises and the conclusions. Calculations are predicated upon assessments; among other things, someone has to decide which items should be included in the calculation and how they should be evaluated. And someone must judge how much money will be invested in gathering information about the uncertain future (Scapens 1985).

Those who make calculations must believe something about the future: how various conditions will play out and what the connections are among various conditions. This is one reason why decision makers who are presented with finished calculations by their colleagues become unsure. Have all the significant items really been included in the calculation? How were various consequences evaluated? It can be difficult for decision makers to penetrate every detail. Those who attempt the task are likely to end up in a 'calculation swamp' – a morass of numbers that can be understood only by endlessly evoking more numbers. Decision makers who find themselves in the swamp are forced to make increasingly detailed assessments and estimations, until they are finally forced to redo the calculation down to the last detail.

That decision makers mistrust the basic values and assessments of their colleagues is not necessarily important, as long as the results of the calculation provide a basis for a decision they like. But if the results of the calculation point towards a decision the decision makers do not like, the situation gets tricky. Few, if any, self-respecting decision makers are capable of making decisions they consider wrong. When the results of the calculation are inconsistent with what they think will be a good decision, these decision makers are torn between what they consider right and their expectations of rationality, which should mean that they rely upon and make decisions in accordance with the results of the calculation. Those who want to make a decision contrary to the calculation results must refer to some technical fault, find additional information that is lacking and that will lead to the decision they want to make, or quite simply ignore the calculation. In either case, they may upset those who performed the calculation. They would have avoided these problems had they not had access to a calculation.

Decision makers use calculations in order to convince others (Jansson 1992). Those who can refer to a calculation have stronger arguments compared to people who merely think or feel – at least that is the general perception. In fact, calculations are based on reasoning, summarized in numbers and not evident in the calculation. People who calculate tend to base their assessments upon what they believe other people consider reasonable. At worst, they make assessments based on wild guesses, imitations of other people's assessments and their own feelings – even though they give the impression of a calculation based on a rational analysis.

Groupthink

Our second example of how a particular decision situation tends to shape decisions has to do with *collective decisions* – decisions made by more than one decision maker. People who belong to an organization are expected to fit in. They should not only obey their bosses, but also align themselves with others who know how to behave in various situations. And they should work to improve their personal capacity to apply the rules established by these people. Many decisions in organizations are made with the goal of creating uniformity and predictability among members of the organization. *Team building* has long been a popular way of creating job satisfaction and obtaining cooperation – getting everyone to 'pull in the same direction'. When decision makers trust that their colleagues know – and like – what applies, it facilitates their decision-making. Many decisions can be delegated or become superfluous.

Members of the organization know how they should behave and what they are supposed to do.

Still, organizational members may become so worried about fitting in (and remaining members of the organization) that they dare not express personal opinions, and they accept decisions that they fundamentally dislike. Members of organizations lose their autonomy because they value the cohesiveness in their organization or their department more highly than they value carefully considered decisions. They may even regard cohesion as so important that it assumes moral overtones (Jackall 1988). Moreover, decision makers may be exposed to such strong group pressure that they lose virtually all their capacity to think realistically about a situation (Janis 1982). The risk that every group member will reason the same way as every other group member is especially high when there are no clear rules for how decisions should be made and the group is subjected to stress. Stress may come from the outside or be created within the organization. It becomes especially palpable when a group has recently failed at a task or when people are expected to make decisions that require expertise that is lacking in the group. Groups confronted with a moral dilemma are particularly prone to stress if they see no alternative to breaching established moral principles.

Janis (1982) identified a phenomenon that he labelled 'groupthink'. It refers to the way group members adjust to each other, to the extent that they dare not express dissenting opinion. They even become incapable of discerning an alternative view, because they believe that the group simply cannot be wrong. They become so sure that they are right that they ignore signals from the outside that should have induced them to reflect and make another decision.

The term 'groupthink' has been used to explain failed decisions in US foreign policy – the escalation of the Korean War, the invasion of Cuba and the protracted Vietnam War (Janis 1982). Later failures in the IT and telecom industry, such as the 'dotcom bubble' and the Enron scandal have also been interpreted as the consequences of strong group pressure (Howard 2011).

Specific symptoms characterize groupthink: Group members experience a sense of invulnerability and imperviousness to setbacks; they believe that their positions are morally legitimate and that there are no differences of opinion within the group. Furthermore, they have stereotypical beliefs about people who do not belong to the group – people they may characterize as saturated with naïve or unrealistic ideals. Self-censorship reigns supreme; group members are subjected to heavy restrains and express no concerns or differences of opinion.

Groupthink entails exaggerated optimism and exaggerated risk taking. The group members do not use their critical minds, but ignore warning signals and accept unethical decisions. Even though decision makers have been specially appointed to make key decisions, which should be based on thorough analysis of all conceivable information, they become so caught up in the situation that they refrain from gathering information.

Unlike team building, groupthink has an overwhelmingly negative ring to it. It is used primarily to describe how people make (as it turns out) disastrous decisions because their thinking processes are too similar (Sims 1992).

Decision makers who aspire to promoting the long-term success of their organizations are confronted with a problem. On the one hand, they must somehow get their colleagues to feel such loyalty and sense of belonging to the organization that they need not hesitate to delegate. On the other hand, they do not want to end up with such malleable colleagues that valuable information is withheld from them. Janis (1982) recommended that prior to every critical decision, decision makers should appoint a devil's advocate tasked with a critical review of the proposed decision, noting its weaknesses and conceivable but overlooked options. Similarly, Hedberg (1976) recommended good 'opponents' who create a certain level of uncertainty about the options that decision makers are considering.

Insistence upon Wrong Decisions

A third example of the difficulties in applying the rules of rational decision-making occurs in a situation in which decision makers refuse to back down once they have made a decision – even if that decision is *obviously wrong*. As important as it is that decision makers make the 'right' decision, it is equally important that they are able to change their minds and make a *new* – and different – decision when they become dissatisfied with an earlier one. That such decisions can be difficult is illustrated by an example from the City of Gothenburg, where the choice was between investing more money in an ambitious biogas project or shutting down the project, thereby accepting that it had cost money but had accomplished nothing. In December 2010, the city decided to invest SEK 1.4 billion (approximately EUR 140 million) in biogas – more than eleven times as much as the Swedish state had invested over two years. But by December 2011, the project was estimated at SEK 300 million (EUR 30 million) more than had been estimated in the previous year. The city then had to choose whether to invest more money or abandon the project and accept the fact that the SEK 700 million (EUR 70 million) already spent on the project could not be recovered. This money represented sunk costs – costs that had been spent and could not be retrieved, no matter what further decisions were made (*Göteborgs-Posten* 2011). The city stuck to its first decision and built Sweden's largest – and most expensive – biogas plant (*Second Opinion* 2014).

Staw and Ross (1987) have suggested a number of reasons that decision makers in these situations find it difficult to change course, accept that the money was spent unnecessarily, and make a new decision that flies in the face of the earlier decision:

- The decision makers believe the evaluation was performed too early; the project has not had enough time to 'settle in'. When more time has passed, everything will go as planned from the outset.
- The decision makers believe that insufficient resources explain the failure. With more effort – and more money – things will work out.
- The decision makers find no alternative to continuing as before.
- The decision makers believe the options they can see ahead will be too costly.
- The decision makers put their hearts and souls into the earlier decision, and a new decision would entail too great a loss in personal status.
- The decision makers have presented the earlier decision as strategically critical, and a new decision would impact the identity of the entire organization.

By using various 'mechanisms of hope' (Brunsson 2006) decision makers can convince themselves and others that their decision was the right one and should not be changed – even if an outside observer recognizes strong indications that the decision has failed to produce the intended outcome. They may simply avoid considering the current outcome; rather they continue using the same supporting arguments they used when making the decision. Or they refer to what they believe are positive consequences with similar decisions in other organizations, indicating that their decision is also the right one. Or they interpret negative information about their own decision in a way that does not challenge the decision. They think that the situation will change to fit the decision – even though it has had no effect or even negative effects to that point, it will turn out to be the right decision in the long run.

Taken as a whole, these factors contribute to decision maker inertia: Once the decision makers have made a decision, a great deal will have to occur before they disavow themselves by making the opposite decision or stop the actions following the previous decision. In the meantime, their perseverance may lead to substantial costs.

RULE-FOLLOWING, IMITATION AND EXPERIMENTATION

Organizations have plenty of rules that regulate what their different members may or must do in various situations. Rules set the preconditions for delegation, because decision makers can rest assured that their colleagues will make the same decisions they would have made (Weber [1924]1964). The history of the organization and the decisions that managers made in the past are also significant: Old decisions live on as 'sediment' in an organization, or it is 'bred in the bone' that various rules should apply.

Rules are a predominant feature of the archetypical state bureaucracy that Max Weber described in the early 20th century (Weber [1924]1964). They create the prerequisites for impartiality: Neither the organization's members nor those they interact with should be accorded special treatment; everyone should be judged and treated in accordance with the relevant rules. Bureaucracy has been criticized and ridiculed and described as rigid and outmoded, especially in popular management and leadership literature. Even Weber was concerned that people would operate as cogs in a machine, constantly in motion, and intent on climbing to ever-higher levels in the organizational hierarchy (Wren 2005).

But it is a rare organization that is entirely void of bureaucratic features. Rules operate as a guarantee against arbitrariness and randomness, both in organizations and in interactions between organizations and their environments. Still, there is risk that decision makers will get bogged down in rules they perceive as self-evident and necessary ('This is what we must do, because this is what we have always done'), but which prove to be outmoded, making it difficult for decision makers to adapt their organizations to new conditions. Organizations identified as bureaucracies have been identified as particularly sluggish (Burns and Stalker 1961).

Organizations have tried to avoid (allegedly) old-fashioned management by substituting objectives for rules. Underlying this idea is an even stronger principle of delegation: Decision makers should state what they want to be achieved in various parts of the organization, but those who work there should decide for themselves how the objectives should be accomplished. Management by objectives then replaces management by rules. This idea has proven difficult to realize, however (Jacobsson et al. 2015). In the Swedish state administration, the government was repeatedly criticized for being far too vague and for providing too little guidance for the operation of the government agencies. Or the government was criticized for being too clear, so that, in practice, it returned to the despicable management by rules (Holmblad Brunsson 2002; Tarschys 2006). Nor was it made clear in advance what would happen if the objectives were not met or if the results exceeded expectations (Brunsson 1997).

When members of an organization are expected to follow rules, their scope to use other decision logics is narrowed. This applies to those who are supposed to lead organizations as well; they follow rules that other organizations have decided upon. Business firms repeatedly complain that laws and ordinances are too numerous and too complicated. The government promises to simplify rules, but is criticized for having failed. But organizations are not simple victims of interfering bureaucracies; they employ special interest organizations and a long line of other lobbyists to influence the scope and design of rules.

Organizations are similarly exposed to external rules when they engage people with specialist expertise. Professional norms for the way various tasks should be performed may be critical to the successful survival of organizations, but they constrain the organizations' freedom to design unique rules for its activities. Physicians, for example, think it is more important to give their patients good advice than to follow the cost-savings rules designed by their health trust.

One reason for the vast number of rules (despite all the talk about deregulation in many contexts) is that alongside central governments that enact laws, ordinances and other rules, there are other organizations – and individuals – who set *standards* for others. Standards are rules that organizations are not compelled to follow, but which many follow voluntarily (Brunsson and Jacobsson 2000). International standardization bodies are setting standards for virtually all products. There are more and more standards for the design of production and management processes. Self-appointed management and leadership experts are trying to design standards for the structure and management of organizations and are launching one management concept after another. In addition, a sea of organizations devoted to defending the environment, justice and human rights are designing standards for these areas.

Decision makers have several reasons to comply with standards, one of which is the possibility of deriving authority from those who have decided on standards. It is easier to convince members of an organization that specific rules should be followed if they are recommended by outside experts rather than being set merely by decision makers in their own organization. Like individuals, organizations that decide to follow certain standards can communicate a particular image of themselves. They may describe themselves as responsible, benevolent organizations, because they follow rules issued by organizations dedicated to improving working conditions in poor countries. Outsiders sometimes rank organizations according to the way they follow various standards – and organizations that place themselves at the top of the ranking list acquire high status.

Imitation

Many of those who set standards or draft recommendations for the management of organizations present stories about organizations that have succeeded, thanks to those standards or recommendations, and others are encouraged to imitate these flourishing organizations (Abrahamson 1996; Røvik 2007). Those who adhere to a particular 'management fashion' find arguments in some standard, but they may also argue that it is a good idea to do like other – obviously successful – organizations do: 'So many cannot be wrong.'

Benchmarking is one explicit method of imitation, in which organizations try to compare themselves with similar organizations in order to improve their own management. The idea has been that all organizations will design their operations in the optimal way as a result of widespread benchmarking. But like other similar management methods, this method has been criticized. What information about an organization's activities is so easily available that others can imitate it? Are the correlations between what is being imitated and the organization's success properly understood (Walgenbach and Hegele 2001)? Organizations that are especially inclined to imitate organizations they perceive to be successful run the risk of obtaining the wrong models and failing. The organizations they are trying to imitate may simply have been unusually lucky (Denrell and Liu 2012).

Experimentation

Sometimes the decision itself becomes a way for organizations to acquire information about how they should have argued or decided; instead of trying to grasp their situation ahead of a decision, they do so after the fact. In these cases, the decision makers learn what they want when they make the decision or after the decision has been made. In this respect, organizational decision makers do not differ all that much from people who make decisions on their own behalf – as discussed in Chapter 2. Like other individuals, they re-examine their preferences and intentions when they see the outcome of their decision; until then, they consider their preferences and intentions as hypotheses of a sort. Instead of making decisions based on forecasts and calculations, they build evidence.

Decision makers who make multiple 'minor' decisions rather than fewer 'major' decisions to institute dramatic changes can limit their analysis. They engage in what Lindblom (1959) called 'the science of muddling through' and use many minor decisions to proceed by trial and error and gradually discover the effects of their decisions.

By muddling through, decision makers are given the opportunity to learn from their experience and change course when they are not satisfied with their decisions. They certainly run the risk of making small mistakes, but they avoid big mistakes because they or those affected by their decisions are given the opportunity to intervene. The decision makers acquire new information or change their minds. Those concerned may contribute observations that show how they were affected by particular decisions, thereby mitigating the risk that significant effects of the decisions will be overlooked. The decision makers are given help in predicting the possible outcomes of their decisions.

The risk that decisions are insufficiently analysed may also be reduced by varied experience and opinions within the organization (and organizational members with the courage to stand up for their views, as Janis suggested in his discussion of groupthink). Those who advocate *evidence-based management* (Pfeffer and Sutton 2006) emphasize that decision makers should take advantage of their organization's experience. Their basic argument is that organizations must seek continuous improvement. But every organization is unique, and every member's special expertise must be utilized. By comparing their decisions with the effects they observe and with the effects of similar, earlier decisions, the decision makers gather evidence.

The recommendations on muddling-through, evidence-based decision-making and experimentation in general, easily become idealistic. It has been popular to talk about 'learning organizations' as special, better kinds of organizations, which improve their odds of success through their learning. The arguments may seem persuasive but are hardly immune to objections. First and foremost, it is by no means certain that decision makers will learn the right things. They may misinterpret their experience and make decisions that impair rather than improve their conditions for success (March and Olsen 1975). If they cannot isolate the effects of many minor decisions, they may draw the wrong conclusions and construct fallacious causality (Levitt and March 1988; March 2010). In this case, they create the information and gain experience that is disadvantageous to their future decision-making.

POST-HOC RATIONALIZATION

Organizational decision makers have reason to rationalize their decisions post-hoc if they want to appear to be in control. Control of future events is what rational decisions express, for what will happen is ultimately controlled by the decision makers' specific preferences. The image of decision makers in control is part of the very definition of organization. It is more difficult for organizational decision makers than for individuals to gain acceptance for the defence that they were just following the rules, that they imitated others that have merely done as they usually do, or that they thought it would be fun to try something a little different. Were decision makers to refer to their intuition or their feelings, they would probably be greeted with either compassion or contempt. And were they to place the blame on coincidence, they would soon find themselves made redundant.

Decision makers may actually try to imagine what others will think when they make their decisions; they reason according to the logic of consequences, but instead of thinking about the benefit the organization will gain by their decision, they imagine what others will say. The future they consider is only indirectly related to the best interests of the organization; more directly, it has to do with their own role as decision makers and the preferences of future observers: Which decision are observers going to like best?

Studies show that decision makers who consider such factors choose options other than those they would have chosen if the benefit to the organization had been foremost in their thoughts. They play it safe, compromise and replace preferences that apply to the best interests of the organization with preferences that include the opinions – or the perceived opinions – of others. Such decision makers are especially keen to show a clear basis for their decision, such as calculations, which they refer to as a means of justifying their decisions (Simonson 1989).

Another possibility is to define a variety of justifications for decision makers to select from later. Returning to Charles Darwin's decision-making process described in Chapter 2, although Darwin probably tried to consider many decision variables, he might, in fact, have used only one: the soft wife on a sofa. In an organizational context, a similar presentation of decision criteria is likely to be a kind of camouflage. The decision makers find it opportune to present numerous reasonable decision criteria; only later, when they know what decision they want to make, do they use one or a few of these criteria to justify their decision. This was the case with a Danish architectural competition for which the summary competition brief was almost 70 pages long, including over 500 criteria that competitors must meet (Kreiner 2012). Yet it was relatively easy for the committee experts to agree on the winner. They had made their decision at an early stage – probably based on their experience. Because there were so many criteria to choose among, it was easy for them to use the competition brief for post-hoc rationalization.

4. The consequences of decisions[1]

Many descriptions of decision processes end with the decision. But what happens after that? Does the decision lead to anyone acting in accordance with that decision? And what consequences do decisions have other than choice and action? We devote this chapter to discussing five consequences of decisions:

- how the decision process affects the capacity of organizations (and individuals) to act;
- how decisions control (or do not control) the actions of others;
- how decisions confer responsibility;
- how decisions produce attention and legitimacy, regardless of whether they are implemented; and
- how decisions facilitate actions that are contrary to the decision.

Our focus in this chapter is on decisions in organizations, but we contend that much of the discussion applies to individual decision-making as well.

DECISIONS AND THE CAPACITY TO ACT

In making decisions, people are trying to make the future less uncertain by confining themselves and others to a specific action. Then no one should need to deliberate further, and the concentration can shift to the action decided upon. Those whose task is to implement decisions will be able to act vigorously, because they know what has to be done.

---

[1]   This chapter draws on Brunsson (2007).

Yet decisions have a tendency to generate uncertainty (Brunsson 1985; Luhmann 2000), because a decision shows that the future could be different. Because the decision is perceived as the choice of one option among many, it illustrates the possibility that decision makers could have chosen another option – even a better one. Maybe they should change their minds. Maybe they will. And it is by no means a given that the uncertainty will subside because the decision makers have brooded a great deal over their decision. The opposite, in fact, may be true.

Uncertainty is no solid foundation for action. People who are unsure about what should be done and what will be done are inclined to keep on deliberating what should actually be done. They become irresolute, and their capacity to do anything slips away. As Shakespeare observed in the 16th century:

> Thus conscience does make cowards of us all,
> And thus the native hue of resolution
> Is sicklied o'er with the pale cast of thought,
> And enterprises of great pith and moment
> With this regard their currents turn awry,
> And lose the name of action.

(*Hamlet*, Act III, Scene 1)

This 'pale cast of thought' is likely still at work today, when people are encouraged to make carefully considered, preferably rational decisions. For a modern online dating site, love is not enough; a future spouse must be the one among hundreds or thousands who best fits the seeker's preferences (Illouz 2007). For the person who reviews all preferences, options and consequences, to seize the day and actually do something becomes an over-whelming task. Chances are that much of life will pass before a decision leads to action. Had Charles Darwin not radically simpli-fied his decision situation, it seems doubtful that he could ever have made up his mind about marriage. (See Box 2.1 for Darwin's decision-making process on whether to marry.) Decisions are not very likely to lead to decisiveness.

The effects of uncertainty are especially serious in organizations. For many organizations, mobilization to action is a key point – getting the members to perform specific actions jointly and in a coordinated manner. And yet coordinated action is one of the most difficult tasks that organizations face. Sometimes it is a matter of 'enterprises of great pith and moment', and it is not always easy in those situations to persuade people to make an effort to achieve something worthwhile together. An industrial business firm must be able to make complex products like cars, computers or sophisticated medical devices. With time, coordinated routines can be developed for the production processes, but the firm must also develop new products for which there are no routines established. In these cases, it depends on the willingness and capacity of employees to make a committed contribution to new, joint projects.

In order for employees to contribute, they need to be relatively certain about expectations. They must feel fairly certain that others have understood the matter in the same way and intend to act accordingly. There is little point in expending energy on projects if one does not believe that others will contribute; nothing is going to come of it anyway. Employees should also be convinced that the project is a good option. Uncertainty in these respects undermines mobilization and, at worst, threatens the organization's survival.

No Decisions

Decision makers who want to prevent their decisions from leading to uncertainty may react in various ways. They may try to convince themselves and others that they have not actually made any decision. They describe the only possible future – a future they cannot affect. What has to be done is 'necessary', and 'the only possible way' – and by no means a matter for decision-making. If this reform is not implemented, the country will end up in economic crisis; if the firm does not manage to develop and market these new products, it will go bankrupt.

Many decision makers argue in this way. If they manage to convince other members of the organization that something is necessary rather than an issue requiring a decision, they increase expectations that a specific change will be implemented. And even if organization members fear that the change has many negative aspects, it is still better than not implementing it. If something is necessary, it must be done, even if it does not appear to have beneficial consequences, or if it conflicts with relevant rules.

Irrational Decision Processes

One argument in favour of the model of rational decision-making is that, arguably, it makes decision makers feel more secure. Those who systematically compare all conceivable options and carefully assess the consequences of those options should feel convinced that the option decided upon is truly the right one. This may be true in some cases, when the decision makers are familiar with a topic and must assess only the immediate future. But there are also decisions with consequences for the distant future – situations in which it is difficult to feel certain about anything, no matter how much work is invested in projections and forecasts. This situation applies to decisions about public investments in infrastructure or corporate decisions about product development, for example. In such situations, rationality exacerbates rather than mitigates uncertainty. Every option studied reminds the decision makers that they could do things another way, and every prediction of consequences and preferences reminds them of the uncertainty of their assumptions about the future. A detailed analysis of all pros and cons merely serves to increase uncertainty about which option is best.

The tendency of decision makers to break the rules of rationality (as described in Chapter 3) can be a reaction to uncertainty. Decision makers who truly want to avoid creating uncertainty can benefit by systematically breaking the rules of rationality. At an early stage, they eliminate all options but one, or they keep obviously bad options in the running; these do not spread uncertainty but may, on the contrary, show how good the main option is compared to the bad ones.

Another way of avoiding uncertainty is to attend to only one type of consequence: The decision makers draw attention to the positive consequences of the option to be implemented and the negative consequences of other options. The decision makers' first impression of an option determines the types of consequences they consider.

For decision makers who base their deliberations on distinct preferences, it may be difficult or impossible to predict all relevant consequences. And the available information may show both positive and negative consequences of each option. For decision makers trying to avoid uncertainty, it is better to start with the consequences and specify the preferences later, which makes it easier to state the preferences that fit the consequences. The decision makers' preferences are then turned into arguments for action rather than criteria for choice.

Decision processes with one or very few options that emphasize the advantages of one option, ignore disadvantages, and adapt preferences to the option the decision makers choose are called *systematically irrational* processes. Such processes reduce uncertainty. The decision makers convince themselves and others that the option they prefer is the only right one, thereby increasing opportunities for vigorous implementation.

Thus irrational decision processes are not necessarily related to decision makers' lack of knowledge or ability to make rational decisions. Irrational decision processes may be the result of a drive to reduce their uncertainty and the uncertainty of others – and the need to feel more certain that the decision will actually lead to action. In organizations and situations in which it is important but difficult to achieve coordinated action, considerable departures from the rules of rationality are to be expected.

Likewise, attempts to *increase* the rationality of decision processes can be seen as attempts to block action. Opinion groups that want to block the implementation of political decisions introduce rational arguments that should be included in a decision process. A group opposed to the building of a road, for example, points to noteworthy interests beyond those that were previously discussed, asserting that more options should be investigated. They suggest other possible routes, or they introduce options that are relatively far removed from the proposed road expansion: a social planning that reduces the need for car travel, for example, or a plan to persuade people to use public transportation instead of cars. They argue that all negative consequences of the proposal have not been considered or thoroughly studied. In short, their arguments indicate that the decision process has not followed the rules of rationality and that a new, more rational decision process is needed. Further study is required! Decision makers have a hard time fending off such arguments, because it requires them to defend their substandard rationality. This type of opposition can sometimes lead to years of study, but no action.

As we previously described, many decision scholars believe that a decision process designed according to the rules of rationality is a good method for discovering the right action to choose. But when, in addition, they recommend rationality as a general principle, they ignore the antagonism between making the right choice and getting things done. Like individuals, organizations are expected to manage both parts. But this is no easy task.

Perhaps, as discussed in Chapter 3, the devil's advocate that Janis (1982) recommended to increase the rationality of decision-making really would prevent many vigorous but foolhardy actions of the type he studied. The problem is that such a person would probably prevent many other actions and, in the worst-case scenario, would prevent any action. The number of entrepreneurs would be decimated if everyone made strictly rational decisions. Considering that most new businesses do not survive long, and that few become highly profitable, there is a risk that rational analysis would make many fledgling entrepreneurs realize that the prospects for their planned business are not particularly good and that they would choose not to take the risk of opening a business (cf the task of writing a doctoral dissertation, as discussed in Chapter 2). That decision may be good for most of them, but bad for society, which would lose the companies and innovations that later proved successful.

The Logic of Appropriateness

Decision makers have the possibility of reducing uncertainty by making decisions based on an existing rule rather than an uncertain future. It is usually easier to agree about what has happened than it is to agree about what is going to happen. Organizations have reason, therefore, to use the logic of appropriateness. They design strategies or policies that contain rules for future decisions. Business firms, for example, develop 'fundamental values' that include rules for their business activities and for social responsibility. They employ strategies for targeting product segments and policies for managing difficult human resource issues. As described in Chapter 3, such rules are often vague and ambiguous. But if they can be made clear, concrete and consistent, they can better serve as the basis for the logic of appropriateness. Ideally, then, the decision makers will have no need to make complex and uncertain forecasts of the outcomes of various options; they can limit themselves to assessing whether the action is consistent with the established rules. Many people will be in agreement and feel certain about the right course of action.

Decision makers may need to use the logic of consequences when they decide to introduce certain rules, which may lead, momentarily, to uncertainty and discord about the rightness of the rules. But if, through the repeated use of the rules, the decision makers can show that the rules, in fact, apply, they can avoid producing uncertainty when making specific decisions.

Fundamental values, policies and strategies are rules defined by organizational decision makers. But something resembling rules may also arise spontaneously in organizations. People who co-operate in an organization develop shared beliefs about the content of the work and how it should be performed, which problems are important, and the state of the organization's environment. They share experiences of what they did in the past, and they develop ideologies – particular ways of perceiving reality.

Shared ideologies often give rise to shared norms – beliefs about how the organization should act in various situations. Norms are rules upon which no one has specifically decided. They make the existing or proposed situation seem obvious. Organizations with strong and shared norms may be easily mobilized into action. Joint and coordinated action is facilitated if everyone who is supposed to participate in an action believes that what should be done is obvious, and knows that others share their view. As the concept of groupthink indicates, however, there is no guarantee that these actions will be the best.

DECISIONS AND MANAGEMENT CONTROL

Organizations are based on the idea that decisions control the activities that are undertaken. But making decisions about what should be done is not the only source of power available to managers. They also have the right to review what other members of their organization do and to verify that their decisions are implemented. Furthermore, they can dole out incentives for compliance and penalties for noncompliance. Yet none of this guarantees that their decisions will always be carried out. The organizational literature suggests that organization members do not let themselves be managed in a predictable way. If decisions are not implemented, the intended order is threatened. Decision makers have power over decisions, but not over actions.

One reason decisions are not implemented is that they produce too much uncertainty by being too rational. Another reason is that the interests of decision makers and their colleagues diverge. Managers of a large organization must consider the interests of external stakeholders and of the entire organization. The people who are supposed to be managed – employees in a firm or a state administration, for example – may seek to safeguard what they consider the best interests of their department or activity, or they may comply with norms related to their profession. In some cases, they accept the goals of the decision makers, but believe that these goals can be accomplished in another, better way. In other cases, they discover that managers are acting more in their own best interests than in the interests of the organization. When this occurs, employees or other organization members do not want to implement the decisions, and they attempt, in various ways, to block the implementation.

Even when people do want to implement a decision, it is not certain that it will be followed by the actions intended by the decision makers. The intentions of decision makers are not always clear. The decision may be formulated so ambiguously or in such general terms that it is open to multiple interpretations (Baier et al. 1986) because that was the only way the decision makers could reach an agreement. Decisions may also conflict with past decisions, a situation which easily produces confusion and entails a risk that none of the decisions will be implemented. Myriad practical obstacles to implementing decisions may arise as well (Barnard [1938]1968; Pressman and Wildavsky [1973]1984). And those who are supposed to implement a decision do not always have the time to implement it then and there. By the time they are able to deal with it, it may already be past its best-by date, and it becomes unclear if the decision is really supposed to be implemented.

Time, Implementation and Dissatisfaction

A further complication is that implementation takes time – sometimes considerable time. If the decision makers' preferences change in the interim, before their decision is implemented, a successful implementation will not lead to an agreement between the organization's actions and the decision makers' preferences. The decision makers were dissatisfied from the outset, so they decided that something new should be done. But they are dissatisfied after the implementation as well – precisely because the implementers were obedient and did what the decision makers decided!

The administrative reforms that are often decided in large organizations serve as one example of the changing preferences of decision makers (Brunsson 2009). New ways of organizing and managing are introduced: Sometimes the organization is centralized and sometimes it is decentralized. Opinions about the way organizations should be managed come fast and furious in the general discussion; they involve management by objectives, quality management systems, process re-engineering or lean production.

Organizational reforms take a long time to implement, and there is considerable risk that the decision makers will be attracted to a new idea in the meantime. Long before a centralization reform is fully implemented, decision makers are likely to realize that centralization has disadvantages, and decentralization becomes more attractive again. Even as they are busy introducing a quality management system, for example, they become enamoured with books and articles about the advantages of lean production. By the time a reform has been implemented, the decision makers have had time enough to change their minds and have already decided on a new reform of different, even contradictory content. They are dissatisfied with how the organization works, both before and after the implementation of a reform.

Thus the implementation of decisions in accordance with the intentions of decision makers will not necessarily lead to satisfied decision makers. The notion that it is easy to couple implementation with satisfied decision makers is based on the assumption that decision makers are slow, whereas implementation is fast. The situation is usually the opposite, however, because thinking is faster than action. Decision makers do not stop thinking merely because they have made a decision. They may swiftly change their minds, acquire new preferences, and make new decisions. The implementation of their decisions takes considerably longer.

Many employees are aware of this problem, and the demand that decision makers adhere to their decisions is standard in organizations. They believe that decision-making should be at least as slow as implementation, so that no one is criticized for having implemented the decision. But although phlegmatic decision makers who refuse to let go of old ideas become well-liked among those who are meant to implement their decisions, they may be criticized and ridiculed by outside observers for being slow witted and for having failed to understand that the present situation demands new ideas and decisions.

The Problem of Determination

Another problem facing decision makers trying to control organizations through decision-making is related to the question of who decides the content of decisions: the decision makers or those who are expected to implement the decision. It seems obvious that decision makers determine the content of their own decisions, but in many cases that is simply not true. The decision makers have a problem determining the content of decisions. Whereas the problem of implementation has to do with decision makers' power over the action, the problem of determination has to do with decision makers' power over the decision.

It is the rare decision maker who is an expert in every aspect of the organization's business. In democratic organizations, it is even a point of pride that the decision makers are representatives for their electors rather than experts. Large organizations employ a raft of experts with extensive education and experience: engineers in IT firms, architects and city planners in municipalities, physicians in health trusts. The experts' key task is to make their expertise available to the decision makers by regularly informing them about developments in their field, which may involve new problems, the need for new action, new opportunities to solve old problems, or the need for more money to solve other problems. The experts are often the ones who recommend that a decision should be made. And they offer their expertise for investigating an issue in greater detail.

Thus, experts are providing most of the information that the decision makers use when they make their decisions. Whether directly or indirectly, the experts define the possible decisions. Although decision makers have their own preferences and try to be autonomous, the expert information may well determine the decisions they make. In response to all the expert knowledge, the decision makers may have nothing more to present than a few general principles or political objectives (or their emotionally laden feeling about what is the 'right' decision). They may find it difficult to oppose a well-founded and detailed argument based on comprehensive knowledge. It is easier for experts to convince non-experts than the other way around (Brunsson and Jönsson 1979). In addition, decision makers need to justify their decisions to outsiders, and it is difficult to defend a decision that is not supported by experts. The experts provide key arguments in favour of the decisions they advocate.

To sum up, in matters in which expertise truly matters, those who are supposed to be controlled may be the very people who control the decision makers. This situation is problematic because it is difficult to detect. Failure to implement a decision is often relatively clear to both decision makers and other observers, but it can be difficult for everyone to understand that people other than the decision makers have determined the content of the decision. And it is hard to do anything about a problem that few people have observed. This is probably one reason why the problem of implementation is discussed more than the problem of determination. Furthermore, one can expect a negative correlation between these problems: For decision makers whose decisions are determined by experts, the likelihood of implementation increases because there is little reason for the experts to oppose decisions that they have actively influenced. If decision makers see no problem getting their decisions implemented, they tend to believe that they have no control problems. Yet they may have the biggest problem of all. Conversely, serious implementation problems may indicate that decision makers have decided autonomously.

Simultaneously influencing the content of decisions and ensuring that they are implemented is a huge challenge for decision makers – and quite an art. Decision-making and power are on equal footing in public discourse, and decision makers are assumed to be powerful. But those who want to be decision makers because they believe this position automatically confers power are easily disappointed. Nonetheless, the belief that decision makers are powerful is significant, because this belief confers responsibility on them.

DECISIONS AND RESPONSIBILITY

Through their decisions, decision makers not only affect other people and future actions; they also affect themselves. Decision makers are assigned responsibility for their decisions and often for the subsequent actions and consequences as well, a situation that sometimes has an impact on their willingness to make decisions and on the content of those decisions.

Responsibility describes the connection between people and actions (Edwards 1969). In western law and moral philosophy, responsibility is allocated to people causing events with their free will. Those who cause something have power – almost by definition. In classical organizational doctrine, the connection between power and responsibility is considered strong: 'Authority is not to be conceived of apart from responsibility', Fayol ([1916]1949, p. 21) asserted 100 years ago. When decision makers in an organization are believed to be powerful, the responsibility of colleagues at lower levels declines (Barnard [1938]1968), and the power of decision makers is accepted precisely because they accept responsibility (Simon [1957]1965). But only a person who genuinely intends to carry out a given action is assigned responsibility for it. People who are forced to do something by other people or external circumstances are relieved of responsibility (Aristotle 1985, Book 3, Ch. 1).

Declaring that one has made a decision is a powerful way of saying that one is a cause of the actions following the decision and has had free choice. Decisions are regularly interpreted as choices of future actions, and, as discussed in Chapter 1, this interpretation is supported by most theorizing about decisions. If people interpret decisions as choices, they will perceive decision makers as responsible. In other words, standard theory not only explains decisions; it impacts the effects of decisions.

Effects of Responsibility

Responsibility can be a heavy and risky burden that decision makers seek to avoid. For this reason, they sometimes try to delay risky or unpopular decisions as long as possible. They hope that decisions will not have to be made or that someone else will make them. Or perhaps conversely, more people want to be involved in making popular and less risky decisions.

Decision processes can be designed in a way that ascribes greater or lesser responsibility to decision makers. If decisions are intended to confer responsibility, it must be clear that a decision has been made and who the decision makers are. Organizations often employ special procedures to make their decisions clear, using meetings with recorded minutes that specify which decisions have been made and by whom. Voting is used not only to determine which decision enjoys majority support; it is also meant to clarify exactly who has made the decision. People who want to avoid responsibility have the option of abstaining or dissenting. If decision makers as a group want to avoid responsibility, they prefer decision processes in which it is not as clear when and by whom the decisions are made. If meetings are not convened, votes cannot be counted, and minutes cannot be recorded. And if a decision is unclear, it lends itself to later interpretation.

Decision makers can try to reduce their responsibility by engaging in post-hoc rationalization. When they assert that they have made their decisions according to the logic of consequences, they assume greater responsibility than they would by saying that they followed rules. Because the logic of consequences is based on the decision makers' preferences, it seems as if they have truly chosen the decisions. Rule following, on the other hand, means that decision makers share responsibility with rule setters. There are two decisions involved: one decision to set the rule and one decision to follow it. Decision makers who have not participated in the decision to set a rule, have less responsibility. Decision makers who comply with standards are assigned less responsibility for their decisions than are decision makers who do not comply with standards (Czarniawska and Joerges 1996; Huczynski 1993). Those who want to assign heavy responsibility to decision makers, however, are normally reluctant to accept decision makers who 'blame the rules'. If the rules are bad, why follow them?

Arguing that one's decision is an imitation of someone else's decision constitutes another attempt at disclaiming responsibility. And referring to experimentation also blurs responsibility, because decision makers can then claim that they have not actually made a choice: They will make the 'real' decision – and choice – only after the outcome of the experiment becomes apparent.

The effects of decisions on responsibility can influence decision content. Decision makers may prefer to assume responsibility for minor decisions, the consequences of which cannot be profoundly negative. As described in Chapter 3, they split decisions on a major change into many small sub-decisions. Behaviour of this kind can seriously dilute responsibility. As a whole, the decisions lead to major change with major consequences, but when accountability is demanded, one truly responsible party is nowhere to be found – only a few people with limited responsibility for one sub-decision or another. When, in addition, the sub-decisions are extensively spread over time, the first decision makers are likely to have moved to other positions in other organizations or retired, making them less vulnerable to criticism.

The more people involved in a decision, the less responsibility is assigned to each individual. One decision maker bears full respons-ibility, but many people diffuse the responsibility. Decision makers who seek responsibility are typically happy to make decisions alone, whereas those who want to avoid responsibility – with the potential for blame – prefer that others participate in their decisions.

Allocation of Responsibility

Even if decision makers try to reduce their responsibility, they will not necessarily succeed. They did, after all, make the decision. People who are intent on demanding responsibility maintain that decision makers have the opportunity to choose. They express themselves in accordance with decision theories that define deci-sions as choices and thereby support the spread of such theories. And they exaggerate the power that decision makers wield; they avoid talking about problems of implementation or determination.

Referendums are sometimes held in nation states, even in coun-tries where governments and parliamentary assemblies normally make all the political decisions. Although politicians present refer-endums as a way of giving power to the people, they are really making the citizenry responsible for the decision.

Many referendums seem to be merely about responsibility allo-cation. The politicians have already made up their minds and when the people vote in a way that the politicians did not anticipate and do not like, their decision is not implemented or another referen-dum is held, in the hope that it will produce the desired result. This scenario has occurred several times in European countries and in referendums with relation to the European Union. But if politicians want to transfer responsibility to the citizenry, referendums must be presented as choices, even when they are not.

The Meaning of Responsibility

When decisions are important instruments for allocating responsibility, they will play a more pivotal role in society than merely constituting choices. By their decisions, the decision makers become responsible for actions, transferring their legitimacy to these actions. It is easier to gain acceptance for actions if people appointed in a due and proper manner decided them. Decisions about major public investments are accepted only if made by democratically elected politicians. Decisions by boards of directors on major changes in a firm are necessary – if not always sufficient – conditions for employees' acceptance of the changes.

Decisions can give meaning to events. By allocating responsibility, decisions can satisfy a human need to explain why things happen: The decision makers and their decisions seem to be the cause. When decision makers are given responsibility, the responsibility of others declines or disappears, and the decision makers become potential heroes and scapegoats. Decisions clarify who should be rewarded and who should be punished. And when discontent is widespread, there is one action to take: Sack the decision makers!

It happens that decision makers make decisions with hindsight, after an organizational action has taken place. Organization members have acted without a decision having been made, and the decision makers now align this action with a decision. Such decisions are not choices; more likely they are made in order to clarify the fact that responsibility resides with the decision makers and to present an image of an organization in order and under control. One advantage of hindsight decisions is that the decision makers can be more certain that the decision is actually consistent with the action (Tolstoy [1869]2017, part II, Ch. 17).

DECISIONS AS OUTPUT

An important but implicit assumption in most decision theories is that decisions are linked to actions, and as we have described, the intention in making a decision may be to choose action, to influence the capacity for action, to control actions or to assign responsibility for actions. But some decisions have consequences that are not linked to actions. Rather they affect the reputation of decision makers and their organizations.

Organizations often describe their values to external and internal parties or what they are doing or planning to do. A key element of their talk consists specifically of presenting decisions, which gives the impression of greater seriousness than does talk without a decision.

Many organizations demonstrate a great number of decisions. The actions, visions, policies or strategies they decide upon are rarely a secret; on the contrary, their decisions are often published in press releases and increasingly comprehensive annual reports. Large organizations have public relations departments, with tasks that include describing to external and internal stakeholders which decisions were made and why. These organizations follow the traditions of political assemblies. Parliaments are careful to communicate by showing off their debates and publishing their decisions (Edelman 1964).

Large organizations rarely have to beg for attention; the mass media evince keen interest in their plans, strategies and programmes. Organizations are surrounded not only by clients, customers, users or financial backers, but also by an audience. Those who evaluate organizations look at what they have achieved, but also at the decisions they have made. Financial audits cover both accounting records and the decisions the organization made with regard to internal control systems. When organizations are certified according to quality or environmental standards, the primary focus is not on the quality or environmental impact of their goods or services, but on the decisions they made concerning various procedures for their internal work (Tamm Hallström 2004).

When Stockholm was named the European Green Capital in 2010, the judging panel referred to a number of the city's 'ambitious objectives' and decisions for its environmental work as much as it did to the relatively clean air in the city and other physical conditions. It was noted, for example, that Stockholm had decided that the city should be fossil fuel-free by 2050 (*Dagens Nyheter* 2009).

Decisions become an output of the organization, similar to products that organizations create in order to make others like and support them. In addition to their goods and services, organizations show off their good decisions. Preferably, these decisions are appreciated as reasonable, morally unassailable and up to date. Decisions that many people appreciate become all the more important for organizations that have acquired a bad reputation, but organizations with good reputations cannot refrain from publishing their popular decisions either. Criticism of organizational actions is often effectively handled by decisions – typically decisions on policies promising that similar mistakes will be avoided in the future.

Decisions are likely to reach more people than actions are. As Machiavelli observed 500 years ago, princes are judged more by appearance than by reality: 'Everyone sees what you appear to be, few experience what you really are' (Machiavelli [1513]1992, p. 47, Ch. XVIII). Typically, few people are directly affected by an organization's actions – by the employment conditions within a business firm, its products or its pollution. Most people are unaware of what organizations do, and must settle for listening to decisions. If there are no competing descriptions, the decisions that organizations communicate are likely to form the beliefs about what they do.

Even those who have direct contact with an organization are largely listeners. Customers do not always have information about a company's suppliers, and suppliers are unfamiliar with corporate tax planning. Like others, these stakeholders must settle for learning about the organization's decisions about ethical procurement, social responsibility or tax policies.

Decisions are cheaper than goods and services, which is one reason why organizations prefer decisions to action. And the connection between the cheap decision and the costlier action need not be strong. Organizations do not always have to do what they decide. To satisfy an interest in good service, an organization may merely publish a decision to become service-oriented. At least for those who have limited personal experience of the service actually provided, the decision may determine their evaluation of the organization. And even if customers personally had a bad experience with the service, a nice policy makes it more likely that they understand it as an exception that does not represent the general truth. The demand for decisions explains why it is not always necessary for organizations to link decisions and actions. To use popular terminology in organizational research, decisions and actions may be 'loosely coupled' or even 'decoupled', without any negative consequences for the organizations concerned (Meyer and Rowan 1977; Weick 1976).

HYPOCRISY

If people value not only what organizations do, but also what they say and decide, organizations can meet the demands imposed on them through talk, decisions or actions. The ability to satisfy demands in various ways becomes critical when the demands that organizations encounter are contradictory. In these cases, talk, decisions and actions may correspond to different demands and also be contradictory. Like individuals, organizations can act contrary to their decisions. They may decide (or talk about) one thing and do exactly the opposite, or they may do one thing and decide (or talk) to the contrary. This kind of behaviour is called hypocrisy.

If many people want free trade and others feel threatened by imports from other countries, a country can maintain custom tariffs but decide to abolish them some time in the future – as the European Union did with tariffs on bananas from Central America. Business firms with products or production processes that are environmentally destructive could decide on a comprehensive environmental policy or even decide to establish an environmental award – as car producer Volvo once did.

The phenomenon of hypocrisy has given rise to a theory on decision-making that departs from those we have addressed so far in this book (Brunsson [1989]2002, 2007; Krasner 1999; Lipson 2007). It implies that decisions systematically conflict with the actions of individuals and organizations.

Decisions as Compensation

Organizations are frequently exposed to conflicting demands. Business firms should not merely be profitable: they should also provide jobs; offer a pleasant work environment; pay their employees well; provide good service to their customers; and contribute to prosperity, export revenues and a higher gross domestic product – without polluting nature or exploiting people or the environment in other countries. Contemporary welfare states should help families, pensioners and farmers and provide aid to developing countries. Low taxes should be combined with costly welfare programmes, good working conditions for police officers and police services to citizens around the clock.

However positive all of these demands may sound, it is no easy task for a firm or a state to satisfy all of them. Success in one respect often creates failure in another. If one demand is met entirely, other demands may be put on the back burner or not met at all (Friedlander and Pickle 1968).

It becomes difficult in this situation for organizations to act in complete agreement with their decisions. To do so would require them to meet certain demands entirely, while leaving others unmet, leading to vociferous protests from those whose demands were not met. It becomes easier to act in a certain direction if the decision points in the opposite direction. Decisions in one direction compensate for actions in the other direction.

From this perspective, the EU decision to reduce the tariff on bananas in the future was a critical prerequisite for continuing to block banana imports from Central America. If the decision to abolish the tariff had not been made, it would have been difficult to maintain it, and protests against the high tariff would probably have become far too strident. A business firm with environmentally destructive production finds it more difficult to keep polluting if it cannot point to decisions on environmental policies and environmental improvements. It is no surprise, then, that liberal governments in Europe that praised a market economy found it easier than leftist governments did to nationalize industries and raise taxes, whereas leftist governments with socialist agendas found it easier to privatize and implement cutbacks in welfare programmes (Garme 2001).

At least the stakeholders of hypocritical organizations are relatively satisfied with the organization. Without hypocrisy, certain stakeholders would be entirely satisfied, while others would be entirely dissatisfied. Those who are for free trade or those who love bananas are unhappy that the tariffs are high, but somewhat comforted by the decision to lower tariffs. Those who want high tariffs are worried about the decision, but can take comfort in the fact that, for now, the tariffs still exist. None of the parties had their wishes entirely met, but there was no reason for any party to be completely dissatisfied.

An organization that fails to behave in a hypocritical manner will find it more difficult to manage a situation rife with conflict than does an organization that successfully masters the art of hypocrisy. And conflict-filled situations will be more easily accepted if hypocrisy is part of the equation. In a world without hypocrisy, strong dissatisfaction with organizations in general would probably be far more common, which is why hypocrisy helps maintain important social institutions (Shklar 1984).

The phenomenon of hypocrisy challenges the decision theories we have discussed previously in this book. According to standard decision theories, there is a special causal relationship between decisions and actions: Decisions in one direction increase the likelihood that an action will be taken in that direction. And according to the theory on decisions as outputs, there may be no link between decisions and actions. In contrast, the theory of hypocrisy assumes a causal relationship between decisions and actions, but the relationship is the inverse from that assumed in standard theories: Decisions in one direction *reduce* the likelihood of corresponding action, and actions in one direction *reduce* the likelihood of corresponding decisions. Decisions and actions are coupled – not loosely coupled or decoupled – but coupled in a way that differs from the assumptions upon which other decision theories are based.

In discussions of decisions and control, a discrepancy between what is decided and what is done is treated as a problem – a problem of implementation. According to hypocrisy theory, however, that very discrepancy is a solution. Hypocrisy makes it easier for organizations to take vigorous action in a particular direction, even when there are numerous opponents to their actions. And it becomes easier to make controversial decisions, because they are compensated by actions contrary to the decision.

The Driving Forces of Hypocrisy

Hypocrisy may constitute a deliberate strategy for certain decision makers, but hypocrisy may also arise in the absence of intent. It may be an active response to conflicting demands, but may also arise as an effect of conflicts.

Proponents of a particular interest in or outside organizations may seek to prevent other interests from being met. A decision on a particular action therefore constitutes a strong incentive for active resistance to the action. At the same time, the decision pacifies those who support the action and believe that the fight is now over. The result becomes a discrepancy between decision and action – hypocrisy. A decision to build a road, for example, may well become the signal that provokes a reaction from the people who oppose the road – while simultaneously appeasing the proponents. The decision mobilizes the opponents who, if they are strong enough, can prevent the decision from being implemented and the road from being built. The result is hypocrisy on the part of the organization that is deciding one thing and doing the opposite.

It is not unusual for organizations to set goals for activities that currently fail to meet certain demands. Such goals are hypocritical by definition, because they express what is *not* being done. For those who set the goals, the aim may be to avoid hypocrisy and eliminate the discrepancy between decision and action. But in practice, decisions about goals facilitate the status quo. For many years, Stockholm City Council maintained that the city's goal was to eventually reduce vehicular traffic in the city centre; in the meantime, traffic increased. Perhaps the decision makers really wanted traffic to decrease, but the goal statement made it easier for people to accept the fact that traffic was increasing; at least, it weakened the arguments of those who opposed increased traffic. After all, a decision had been made to decrease traffic – eventually. In a similar vein, the 2016 decision to ban polluting automobiles in Mexico City, Paris, Madrid and Athens in 2025 probably makes it easier to obtain acceptance for the present state of pollution (*The Guardian* 2016).

Sometimes goals are expressed in monetary terms. If a government is not willing to spend money on a problem, it can decide to allocate money to the problem four years ahead, in the next election term, thus showing its compassion for the issue, but without committing the present government.

Stability and Instability

Hypocrisy can be unstable. Many people presume that decisions lead to corresponding actions, at least in the long term. They believe that goals are met eventually and expect that in the long term, people and organizations practice what they preach. When that is the case, morally high-flown talk and decisions are a step towards equally decent actions (La Rochefoucauld [1665]2012). Sometimes, these assumptions turn out to be true.

But hypocrisy can also be stable – as has been the case with nation states that unfoundedly asserted sovereignty for more than 200 years (Krasner 1999). Change helps organizations maintain stability: When decisions are designed to be implemented long after they were made, most people will believe that the situation has changed so much that the old decisions are no longer relevant or justifiable. The current situation must be evaluated based upon its own premises. And the old decision makers have probably been replaced with new ones.

Or decisions may be forgotten – probably a common phenomenon. It even happens in parliaments, although parliamentary decision-making constitutes an essential part of that organization's activities, decisions are entered into the record, and various parties have an interest in reminding others of the decisions that were made (Brunsson 1998).

If organizations are reminded of earlier decisions that have not been implemented, however, they may react by once again engaging in hypocrisy. Olson (1996) reported on one example of a city administration that responded to simultaneous demands for a balanced budget and increases in municipal services, by deciding in favour of budget cutbacks, while costs were rising alarmingly. When the poor finances were noticed and criticized, the city made new and even more forceful decisions on budget cutbacks. But in reality, costs continued to rise. This pattern was repeated for several years.

The Impact of Theory

A prerequisite for successful hypocrisy is that people keep track of the decisions that organizations make and what they do. Those who believe in the intrinsic value of both decision and action become receptive to hypocrisy, because their interests are met through both decisions and actions. Materialists, on the other hand, are interested only in what organizations do. But even they pay heed to decisions if they believe in decision theories that describe decisions as choice. They will care about decisions because they believe that decisions increase the likelihood of corresponding action. Thus, hypocrisy works in their case as well. The theory of hypocrisy applies because people do not believe in it, but believe in decision theories with contrary assumptions. This is yet another example of the ways in which decision theories can have significant social effects: They generate responsibility, but they also enable hypocrisy.

Hypocrisy will not work, however, for materialists who believe in the theory of hypocrisy rather than other decision theories. For them, decisions cannot compensate for the opposite actions. If everyone was a materialist and believed in the theory of hypocrisy, the theory would no longer be valid. People would certainly care about decisions, but they would fear that decisions in a certain direction would prevent the corresponding action. It would not be possible to compensate for action with decisions.

It is often difficult to know whether the theory of hypocrisy or standard decision theories apply in a specific situation. Decisions sometimes impede action, which is consistent with the theory of hypocrisy; but sometimes the other theories are right, and decisions facilitate action. This creates difficulties for those who want to influence organizational action – whether lobbyists, external opinion groups or individual participants in decision processes. If there were never any risk of hypocrisy, lobbyists could always focus their efforts on persuading organizations to decide in favour of the actions that the lobbyists prefer. If there is risk of hypocrisy, however, their attempts may have the opposite effect: Lobbyists who successfully persuade decision makers to make what they consider to be the right decision risk impeding or preventing the realization of the action they want. Will a decision to set gender equality targets and establish a gender equality department promote the hiring of more women for executive positions in a company, or will it have the opposite effect? At the United Nations' Climate Change Conference in Copenhagen in December 2009, a proposal was presented calling for nations to commit to a lowering of total carbon emissions by 20 per cent by 2020 – eleven years later. The conference failed, in the sense that the delegates refrained from deciding in accordance with this proposal. Six years later, the states agreed on another deal at a meeting in Paris: The emissions of warming gases were to decrease to zero during the last part of this century – 34 years later at the earliest. Which meeting was most successful from a climate perspective? According to most decision theories, the odds that action against carbon emissions would really be taken declined in Copenhagen and increased in Paris. But according to the theory of hypocrisy, the odds are reversed. In the absence of any decision on long-term targets, the pressure that something has to be *done* about emissions, and sooner rather than later, increases, while a forceful decision to do something in 34 years is likely to be a hindrance for radical action now. Environmental activists who believe in the standard decision theories should have lobbied for a decision in accordance with the proposals, while those who believe in the theory of hypocrisy should have lobbied against them. For the standard decision theorists, the Copenhagen meeting was a failure and the Paris meeting was a success; for the hypocrisy theorists, it was the other way round.

5. Complex decision processes

The various consequences of decisions that we have described complicate all sorts of decision-making, especially decision-making in organizations, where many people are either involved or affected. Many experienced decision makers probably realize that decisions have both unwanted and unexpected consequences, which should affect their willingness to make decisions and reduce the number of total decisions made. Decisions lose their attraction if the decision makers fear:

- that they will be forced to choose an option they dislike;
- that the likelihood is that something they wish for declines;
- that the wrong people will be held responsible; or
- that a decision threatens the reputation of the organization.

Decision makers may realize that they do not need to make a decision in order to choose or get something done. If they want to avoid personal responsibility, they could try to get others to make the decisions.

Different decision makers have different goals for their participation in a decision process. Some people want to get something done quickly; others consider the right choice to be more important than the timing; yet others seek to allocate responsibility or improve the organization's reputation. Some people believe that a decision increases the likelihood of action; others believe the opposite. Different decision makers may be inclined to apply different decision logics: Some think in accordance with the logic of consequences, others employ the logic of appropriateness; still others imitate or prefer to experiment. When such differences occur, decision processes become complex and extremely confusing to both participants and outside observers. They become particularly confusing to those who assume that there is only one logic – the logic of consequences – and to those who believe that decisions involve only choice. When several organizations are involved, it is not always clear when a decision was made or by whom.

WHEN ARE DECISIONS MADE?

Poet and novelist Johannes Anyuru (2012, p. 54) described politics as a sort of maze, 'a house in which doors and walls switch places'. Similarly, scholars speak of 'windows' that are opened and closed depending upon the actions of various special interest groups: if they judge that the time is ripe to actualize a problem, and if they think it is worth the effort to bring about a solution to a specific problem (Kingdon 1984). In complex political decision processes, many people have a favourite solution before any problem that fits this solution has arisen. Many conclude that decisions are all about *timing* and argue that one must strike while the iron is hot. The entire decision process then becomes relatively random, departing in a non-systematic way from decided procedures. Above all, there is a lack of the orderliness that characterizes rationality, which starts with the problem to be solved in an optimal way.

The need for a decision is sometimes obvious because decision-making is a routine process. This is true, for example, of decisions about annual budgets. Or something unexpected occurs that every-one thinks decision makers *must* react to. But many times, the situation is not clear-cut. Troublesome signals arrive, suggesting that all is not right with the world. It seems that something is about to happen, and decision makers must decide either to intervene – perhaps with new decisions – or to ignore the signals. If the decision makers find that the signals indicate a problem, they are likely to see some kind of decision in the future. Problems arise, for example, when fundamental values are threatened or when the general opinion is that things are deteriorating. In such cases, the problems become more or less important, depending upon how they happen to be categorized.

Who decides what should be categorized as issues that require decisions? Journalists and lobby organizations have significant influence over the issues that are actualized in governments and large business firms. The media are referred to as the 'fourth estate', which shows that they are ascribed critical importance, in parallel with executive, judicial and legislative powers. Social media influences specific issues to an unwarranted degree. Facebook members and Twitter groups discuss problems in self-reinforcing bubbles, which are eventually brought to the attention of many people and induce reactions from politicians and other expert decision makers, who must react – even to disinformation and obvious lies (Pariser 2012).

But it also happens that issues that were only recently thought to be in need of an immediate decision are suddenly no longer important. There are several possible explanations, and one is that the decision makers and others tire of the issue. The decision process had ground on far too long; there is nothing more to add, and things seem to be going fine without a decision. People get used to a situation that was previously thought to justify intervention; they come to regard as normal something that they previously regarded as distressing or abnormal. Or perhaps the worrying signals fade away. Nor is any decision necessary if public opinion shifts or if the citizenry starts worrying about other things.

One issue may be pushed aside by another. Decision makers are incapable of dealing with an unlimited number of issues simultaneously. If an important problem arises, it is likely that something else will have to be placed on the back burner, at least for the present. In this case, as discussed in Chapter 3, the same constraints apply to decision makers in complex political processes as apply to decision makers in general. There is room for only one scandal at a time. When highly ranked civil servants are found to be corrupt or conspicuously incompetent, the long-term (eternal) question of insufficient resources for the preservation of natural resources becomes less urgent, and debates and decisions can be postponed.

Finally, decision makers are not forever. New top managers, politicians or civil servants with other priorities on their agendas may actually find that the situation their predecessors sought to change does not need to be changed at all – that this is how it should be.

WHICH ORGANIZATION MAKES THE DECISION?

Decision processes become especially complex when numerous organizations are involved and organizations – or individuals – with different tasks, positions and interests try to influence the process. This is typical for many hot political issues. When several political bodies are involved, and many individuals or groups want to make their opinions known, the factors the decision makers should consider in the debate proliferate. A single action may depend upon decisions in several organizations, and many people demand that political parties, municipalities, government authorities, parliament or the government should make certain decisions. Because these organizations are seldom able or eager to address every issue under the sun, they try to get some other organization to make the decision or try to keep the decision from coming up on the political agenda at all.

Several organizations may be involved in the same decision, with little interaction. Jacobsson (1987) showed how events played out when a decision to build a coal-fired energy plant in Stockholm emerged. He found that three parallel decision processes were going on simultaneously. One decision process had a technical orientation and occurred mainly in the city-owned energy company in Stockholm, which was responsible for handling such questions. Another decision process concerned environmental policy and was designed as a dialogue between leading city politicians in Stockholm and civil servants from various government agencies. A third process dealt with national energy policy and engaged politicians and civil servants on the national level.

The various decision processes were based on the discrete preferences of the decision makers in each process; there was no process whereby all preferences combined and were considered simultaneously. That the power plant was finally built and designed in a particular way could be explained based only on what happened overall in the three decision processes. Most of the decision makers, however, were active in only one of the processes. They had insight only into the process in which they were personally involved and had a difficult time understanding why things turned out as they did.

Which organizations are involved in the decision-making determines which options are considered and the content of the decisions. The Tax Agency is expected to consider other options and make decisions other than those made by the Environmental Protection Agency. Where a matter ends up determines how it is defined and the context into which it is placed. This, in turn, has impact on the decision made. But many issues fit multiple organizations, and in these cases, various stakeholders may attempt to steer them to the organization they believe is most amenable to their own solution to a problem – while the organizations do their best to move the problem to somebody else.

A book that characterized the government of Sweden as a decision-making machine reiterated the story of how an infrared white cane for blind people triggered car alarms (Brunsson et al. 1990). A citizen who found this issue disturbing and wanted a change in either the canes or the alarms first phoned the municipal Health Care Inspector. The inspector referred the citizen to the state Environmental Protection Agency, which referred her to the non-governmental organization, Swedish Automobile Association, which referred her to the governmental Transport Safety Agency, which referred her to the Ministry of Transportation, which transferred the matter to the Ministry of Agriculture, which sent the matter for consultation to the governmental Consumer Agency and subsequently decided that the municipality was probably responsible for the issue. The municipal Health Care Inspector now tried to refer the citizen to the police, who referred her to the Ministry of Justice, which handed the matter to the Ministry of Transportation, where it now showed up for the second time. Finally, that ministry responded that the problem would probably work itself out when better products came onto the market. No one wanted to make a decision, and the solution was to let time – and a future inventor – deal with the problem.

In other cases, the situation is reversed and several organizations want to get involved and influence future decisions. Many political issues are relevant to more than one policy area. They may be important to employment, business, environmental policy, tax policy and distribution policy – all at once. When a decision process seems to be ending in a decision that satisfies some people but not everyone, decision makers and special interest groups that want something else intervene. A decision that most people believe is obviously right from the environmental perspective may be debatable from other perspectives. Thus, those who want to oppose a forthcoming environmental policy decision may have more success if they do not get bogged down in environmental arguments, but instead bring up preferences, rules and models that are important to other stakeholders. The more arguments of various kinds they manage to insert into the debate, the more difficult things become for the decision makers: the environmental arguments are important, but in this situation we must consider employment – and not least importantly, tax revenues and the surplus target for central government finances. If many aspects of an issue are brought to the fore, the decision makers become overloaded with information and paralysed, and no decision is made.

Those who want to push an issue in order to induce a particular decision have to handle all these arguments. They had better not concentrate on one policy area, but must proactively emphasize that their preferred decision has no or positive effects in other areas. An environmental organization that wants to see a decision that they consider significant for the environment should try to show that the option they support will have no negative consequences in other areas – that it will not increase unemployment, lead to more complex tax collection or exacerbate income inequalities – maybe even provide benefits in those areas. Perhaps the strongest argument in favour of the environmental organization's suggestion has to do with something other than the environment – an area such as tax policy, in which an environmental organization has no authority. Perhaps it entails a radical simplification of taxation? In that case, specialists from other areas may be engaged in the discussion – and become crucial allies. It could turn out to be the tax experts who ultimately pursue the issue that was actualized by the environmental organization in the first place. The environmental arguments are still there, but they are not as apparent once the issue has been defined as a matter of fair taxation.

In summary, the complexity of decision processes paves the way for collaboration among different groups that share few, if any, values. Such collaboration does not make it easier for outsiders to understand what is happening and why decisions finally turn out as they do. In an open society with open decision processes, in which many people are afforded the opportunity to stick their fingers in the pie, decision-making frequently becomes more opaque than transparent.

After the tsunami

When something unforeseen happens, the ability of organizations to adapt to new – and previously unknown – conditions is put to the test. The situation becomes especially precarious if the unforeseen event affects multiple organizations located in different countries. And things become extraordinarily difficult if the unforeseen event occurs during a holiday, when many responsible officials are off duty and away from home. This was precisely the situation that prevailed after the tsunami disaster in Southeast Asia on December 26, 2004 – Boxing Day.

We allow the decisions and actions that occurred shortly after the tsunami to illustrate many of the arguments we have raised in this book. We use information and assessments found in the main report from the Disaster Committee of 2005 (SOU 2005:104) and concentrate, as the Committee did, on the decisions and actions of Swedish authorities. We begin by reproducing a conclusion from the Committee's afterword (p. 349):

> The tsunami was a natural disaster. It was beyond human power to prevent. Its magnitude, where it would strike and when it would occur could not be controlled. There is no one to blame.

THE QUESTION OF RESPONSIBILITY

Although no one was to be held responsible for the tsunami, the Swedish Committee argued that Prime Minister Göran Persson had overall responsibility for shortcomings in the ability of the government offices to manage and analyse information that the Committee had found – and to act upon it.

There were no extenuating circumstances. When the tsunami disaster occurred, Göran Persson had been prime minister for more than eight years. The matter of a national disaster management organization had been raised several times during his tenure, but the issue had been left up to the government to decide.

The Committee's criticism may be interpreted to mean that the responsibility of decision makers grows with time. The longer someone has had the role of decision maker, the greater this person's opportunities to set a personal stamp on the organization. A recently elected prime minister might have been judged less harshly. Göran Persson's actions, on the other hand, may be interpreted as a matter of attention: The prime minister had many urgent problems to deal with. He did not have time to attend to the risk of extremely unlikely outcomes. For this reason, normal procedures characterized activities after the tsunami.

NORMAL PROCEDURES APPLY

The Committee gave many examples of the way politicians and civil servants initially adhered to the procedures to which they were accustomed. Although the travel providers claimed that they had requested assistance by the evening of December 26, the prime minister declared at a press conference on December 27 that the government required a request from travel providers before it could consider any publicly financed operations to transport Swedish citizens home. The Ministry for Foreign Affairs also included financial considerations in its assessment of arranging the evacuation to Sweden, referring to the taxpayers and suggesting that it might be sufficient to evacuate people to other cities in Thailand.

The Swedish Embassy in Bangkok waited for instructions from the Ministry for Foreign Affairs before taking any extraordinary measures; the embassy's regular staff members were familiar with applicable rules. Initially, they adhered to the normal requirements for passports and the policy that tourists should pay for their own return travel.

The National Board of Health and Welfare stood by its opinion that it was not an operational agency, thereby delaying the responses by two days. The responses of the Rescue Services Agency were delayed as a result of territorial disputes between and within various ministries, and civil servants who bypassed their immediate (but absent) managers and made their own decisions were reprimanded for doing so.

The Committee showed that there were rules and procedures that staff members had difficulty departing from – in both the government offices and government agencies. Perhaps they presumed that these rules and procedures would work even under exceptional conditions. Perhaps they were reluctant to take risks. (And with good reason, as it emerged, given the reprimands received by those who departed from normal procedures.) Or were they so moulded by rules and procedures that their own judgement had been knocked out of order? Did they lack sufficient imagination to understand how they should behave in order to facilitate adjustment to an emergency?

WAIT ... AND SHIFT THE RESPONSIBILITY

The tendency to wait initially and, if possible, shift the responsibility to someone else can also be categorized as normal behaviour.

The Ministry for Foreign Affairs in Stockholm was notified at 04:40 Swedish time, when the Swedish Embassy in Thailand phoned the ministry's consular duty officer at home. The duty officer soon realized that as many as 30,000 Swedes might be in Thailand. The seriousness of the situation was confirmed at 05:30 when the embassy phoned again.

The first call from a member of the public to the Ministry for Foreign Affairs came between 05:30 and 05:40 Swedish time. The caller had received a phone call from a relative who had told them about waves that had swept everything along in their path – trees, cars and hotels – and that there were dead people everywhere. Several similar reports arrived soon after. People wanted to know what they should do. They were told that the ministry had no information about what had occurred and were advised to contact SOS International if they required special assistance. Otherwise, they should contact the Swedish Embassy in Bangkok or wait for the rescue operations mounted by the Thai authorities. At his press conference on December 27, the prime minister also noted that the travel providers had primary responsibility for rescue and evacuation operations.

The first reaction, therefore, was to wait for more information; those who asked for advice and assistance were referred to organizations with a mandate to assist with accidents and minor emergencies. Initially, responsibility lay elsewhere. Was this once again a matter of timid civil servants, disinclined to assume responsibility? Or was this reaction associated with the initial misjudgement of the situation by politicians and civil servants involved?

EXPERIENCE MAKES THE DIFFERENCE

The civil servant who was first informed about the tsunami made amazingly accurate assessments of what had happened. Information could also be sought at an early stage in the online editions of Swedish newspapers or via international TV channels. Other civil servants and politicians misjudged the seriousness of the situation.

When the ministry's other duty officers were contacted early in the morning of December 26, they judged that there was no need for them to interrupt their Christmas holiday and hotfoot it back to their offices in Stockholm on Boxing Day. At 07:30, the operating commander of the Rescue Services Agency judged that a Swedish rescue operation to save lives in a region far from Sweden was pointless. The prime minister perceived the disaster as a humanitarian aid issue and did not contact any other European head of government on Boxing Day.

The Committee argued that in an emergency, people act with the help of a cognitive diagram, a 'map of reality' based on previous experience. Some of those who received early information about the tsunami disaster made associations with the Estonia disaster of 1994. They reacted by quickly trying to organize various kinds of response. But others made associations with the earthquake in Bam, Iran in 2003 or to the 9/11 of 2001 attack and decided to wait and see. They considered circumstances that can be described in hindsight as irrelevant.

IRRELEVANT CONSIDERATIONS DISRUPT THE WORK

The Committee argued that the fact that the central government administration is divided by sector rather than geographical area may lead to lack of clarity from time to time, as to the ministry or government agency responsible for a specific issue. Such matters can normally be cleared up through discussions or negotiations, the Committee declared, although this process can take time. Matters that involve one party's word against another's (such as the question of whether the travel providers had really asked the government offices for assistance) are usually resolved this way as well. But in emergencies, there is no time for territorial disputes. The Committee showed how the work came to be characterized by confusion and perplexity, lack of imagination and lack of empathy. Vague allocation of responsibility, insufficient capacity and competency in the ministries, and absent managers led to unnecessary – and devastating – delays.

The Committee's report included examples of how staff members at the Ministry for Foreign Affairs were more concerned about their own work situations than they were about providing accurate information. Even though family members and the mass media were reporting dead and missing Swedes, the ministry's official position was the initial statement that there were no Swedish citizens confirmed dead in the region. When a civil servant from the Swedish Embassy in Bangkok confirmed in a radio interview that two Swedes had died, the Ministry for Foreign Affairs in Stockholm reprimanded him for threatening to increase the load on the already overloaded switchboard. Out of personal consideration for the Minister for Foreign Affairs, she was not informed of the discussions about helping people in the region. (The minister had apparently been forced to manage a laborious consular matter in the last few days before Christmas.)

The Committee stated that those who misunderstood the situation and initially tried to apply normal decision processes made decisions that could be criticized in hindsight but which, under other circumstances, might have been perceived as minor departures from established procedures. Perhaps these departures – as in the case of the exhausted Minister for Foreign Affairs – were perceived as examples of compassionate concern.

THE SOLUTION: CENTRALIZATION AND A SOPHISTICATED LOGIC OF APPROPRIATENESS

The Disaster Committee found that people need to act in emergencies before they have absolute certainty about the appropriate procedure. It is a mistake to rely on detailed planning systems or preventive measures. In parallel, information and communication become extraordinarily critical. The Committee found that a central government administration must be prepared in such situations to gather, analyse and distribute a great deal of information quickly.

The Committee's sharpest criticism applied to the government offices and the lack of an organization for managing serious emergencies. The Committee therefore proposed that the task of preparation for unforeseeable events should be performed by a new organization – a centrally located disaster management organization that would help to create order in emergency decision-making. The disaster management organization would be characterized by simplicity. Matters of allocation of responsibility and information management would be clarified in advance. The Committee recommended a standard of prudence by which the members of the organization – or all state civil servants – should act rather than remain passive in uncertain situations.

In urgent situations, action is more important than decision.

References

Abrahamson, Eric (1996), Technical and aesthetic fashion. In B. Czarniawska and G. Sevón (eds), *Translating Organizational Change*. Berlin: de Gruyter, pp. 117–138.

Ahrne, Göran and Brunsson, Nils (2008), *Meta-organizations*. Cheltenham, UK and Northampton, MA, USA: Edward Elgar Publishing.

Ahrne, Göran and Brunsson, Nils (2011), Organizations outside organizations: The significance of partial organization. *Organization*, *18* (1), pp. 83–104.

Anyuru, Johannes (2012), *En storm kom från paradiset*. Stockholm: Norstedts.

Aristotle (384–322 BC) (1985), *Nicomachean Ethics*. Indianapolis: Hackett.

Bachrach, Peter and Baratz, Morton S. (1970), *Power and Poverty: Theory and Practice*. New York, NY: Oxford University Press.

Baier, Vicki E., March, James G. and Saetren, Harald (1986), Implementation and ambiguity. *Scandinavian Journal of Management Studies*, *2*, pp. 197–212.

Barnard, Chester ([1938]1968), *The Functions of the Executive*. Cambridge, MA: Harvard University Press.

Beckman, Svante (1983), *Tidsandans krumbukter: Kartor över västerländsk värderingsterräng*. Delrapport från projektet "Värderingsförskjutningar i det svenska samhället", sekretariatet för framtidsstudier. Stockholm: Liber.

Beckman, Svante (1990), *Utvecklingens hjältar: Om den innovativa individen i samhällstänkandet*. Stockholm: Carlsson.

Berger, Peter, Berger, Brigitte and Kellner, Hansfried (1974), *The Homeless Mind: Modernization and Consciousness*. New York, NY: Vintage Books.

Boltanski, Luc and Thévenot, Laurent ([1991]2006), *On Justification: Economies of Worth*. Princeton, NJ: Princeton University Press.

Borges, Bernhard, Goldstein, Daniel G., Ortmann, Andreas and Gigerenzer, Gerd (1999), Can ignorance beat the stock market? In G. Gigerenzer, P.M. Todd and the ABC Research Group (eds), *Simple Heuristics that Make Us Smart*. Oxford: Oxford University Press, pp. 59–71.

Brunsson, Karin (1997), *Ramar, regler, resultat: Vem bestämmer över statens budget?* Rapport till Expertgruppen för studier i offentlig ekonomi, Ds 1997:79.

Brunsson, Karin (1998), Non-learning organizations. *Scandinavian Journal of Management*, *14* (4), pp. 421–432.

Brunsson, Karin (2007), *The Notion of General Management*. Copenhagen: Copenhagen Business School Press.

Brunsson, Karin (2016), A dual perspective on management. *Athens Journal of Business and Economics*, *2* (3), pp. 291–302.

Brunsson, Karin (2016), Organizational change in intrusive and non-intrusive environments. *Journal of Organisational Transformation & Social Change*, *13* (1), pp. 26–42.

Brunsson, Karin (2017), Regulating interest-free banking. In A-K. Stockenstrand and F. Nilsson (eds), *Bank Regulation, Effects on Strategy, Financial Accounting and Management Control*. New York: Routledge, pp. 130–156.

Brunsson, Karin (2017), *The Teachings of Management, Perceptions in a Society of Organizations*. Cham, Switzerland: Springer International Publishing AG.

Brunsson, Karin, Sonnerby, Claes and Wittenmark, Lars (1990), *Beslutsmaskinen: En bok om regeringskansliet*. Lund: Studentlitteratur.

Brunsson, Nils (1985), *The Irrational Organization: Irrationality as a Basis for Organizational Action and Change*. Chichester: Wiley.

Brunsson, Nils ([1989]2002), *The Organization of Hypocrisy: Talk, Decisions and Actions in Organizations*. Copenhagen: Copenhagen Business School Press.

Brunsson, Nils (2006), *Mechanisms of Hope*. Copenhagen: Copenhagen Business School Press.

Brunsson, Nils (2007), *The Consequences of Decision-Making*. Oxford: Oxford University Press.

Brunsson, Nils (2009), *Reform as Routine. Organizational Change and Stability in the Modern World*. Oxford: Oxford University Press.

Brunsson, Nils and Jacobsson, Bengt (eds) (2000), *A World of Standards*. Oxford: Oxford University Press.

Brunsson, Nils and Jönsson, Sten (1979), *Beslut och handling: Om politikers inflytande på politiken*. Stockholm: Liber.

Brunsson, Nils and Sahlin-Andersson, Kerstin (2000), Constructing organizations: The example of public sector reform. *Organization Studies*, *21* (4), pp. 721–746.

Burns, Tom and Stalker, G.M. (1961), *The Management of Innovation*. London: Tavistock.

Cohen, Michael D., March, James G. and Olsen, Johan P. (1972), A garbage can model of organizational choice. *Administrative Science Quarterly*, *17*, pp. 1–25.

Cyert, Richard M. and March, James G. ([1963]1992), *A Behavioral Theory of the Firm*. Englewood Cliffs, NJ: Prentice Hall.

Czarniawska, Barbara and Joerges, Bernward (1996), Travels of ideas. In B. Czarniawska and G. Sevón (eds), *Translating Organizational Change*. Berlin: de Gruyter, pp. 13–48.

Dagens Nyheter (2009), Europas miljöhuvudstad 2010. December.

Dagens Nyheter (2013a), Alla har rätt att behandlas som individer. Headline, February 7.

Dagens Nyheter (2013b), Idag är jag den jag egentligen är. Advertisement Itrim, January 7.

Dagens Nyheter (2013c), Helena af Sandeberg: "Jag har blivit den Helena jag var från början". January 13.

Denrell, Jerker (2012), Mechanisms generating context-dependent choices. In A. Lomi and J.R. Harrison (eds), *The Garbage Can Model of Organizational Choice: Looking Forward at Forty*. Bingley, England: Emerald, pp. 65–97.

Denrell, Jerker and Liu, Chengwei (2012), Top performers are not the most impressive when extreme performance indicates unreliability. *PNAS*, *109* (24), pp. 9331–9336.

Due, Jesper and Steen Madsen, Jørgen (1996), Forligsmagerne. De kollektive forhandlingers sociologi. Copenhagen: Jurist- og Økonomforbundets forlag.

Duhigg, Charles (2016), *Smarter, Faster, Better, The Secrets of Being Productive*. London: Penguin Random House.

Edelman, Murray (1964), *The Symbolic Uses of Politics*. Urbana, IL: University of Illinois Press.

Edwards, Rem B. (1969), *Freedom, Responsibility and Obligation*. Den Haag: Martinus Nijhoff.

Elam, Ingrid (2012), *Jag: En fiktion*. Stockholm: Bonniers.

Elias, Norbert ([1939]2000), *The Civilizing Process* (Über den Prozess der Zivilisation). Oxford: Blackwell.

Fayol, Henri ([1916]1949), *General and Industrial Management* (Administration industrielle et générale). London: Sir Isaac Pitman & Sons.

Finucane, Melissa L., Alhakami, Ali, Slovic, Paul and Johnson, Stephen M. (2000), The affect heuristic in judgments of risks and benefits. *Journal of Behavioral Decision Making, 13* (1), pp. 1–17.

Fischhoff, Baruch (1975), Hindsight ≠ Foresight: The effect of outcome knowledge on judgment under uncertainty. *Experimental Psychology: Human Perception and Performance, 1* (3), pp. 288–299.

Follett, Mary Parker ([1918]1998), *The New State: Group Organization the Solution of Popular Government.* University Park, PA: Pennsylvania State University Press.

Follett, Mary Parker (1941), *Dynamic administration: The collected papers of Mary Parker Follett.* Edited by Henry C. Metcalf and L. Urwick. New York, NY: Harper & Brothers.

Fournier, Susan (1998), Consumers and their brands: Developing relationship theory in consumer research. *Journal of Consumer Research, 24*, pp. 343–372.

Friedlander, Frank and Pickle, Hal (1968), Components of effectiveness in small organizations. *Administrative Science Quarterly, 13* (2), pp. 289–304.

Frykman, Jonas (1988), Fördelen med att vara informell: Konsten att få ett övertag och behålla det. In O. Löfgren (ed.), *Hej, det är från försäkringskassan! Informaliseringen av Sverige.* Stockholm: Natur & Kultur.

Garme, Cecilia (2001), *Newcomers to Power: How to Sit on Someone Else's Throne: Socialists Conquer France in 1981; Non-socialists Conquer Sweden in 1976.* Uppsala: Acta Universitatis Uppsaliensis.

Gigerenzer, Gerd and Goldstein, Daniel G. (1999), Betting on one good reason: Take the best and its relatives. In G. Gigerenzer, P.M. Todd and the ABC Research Group (eds), *Simple Heuristics that Make Us Smart.* Oxford: Oxford University Press, pp. 75–96.

Gigerenzer, Gerd and Todd, Peter M. (1999), Fast and frugal heuristics: The adaptive toolbox. In G. Gigerenzer, P.M. Todd and the ABC Research Group (eds), *Simple Heuristics that Make Us Smart.* Oxford: Oxford University Press, pp. 3–33.

Gladwell, Malcolm (2005), *Blink: The Power of Thinking About Thinking*. New York, NY: Little, Brown and Co.

Goldstein, Daniel G. and Gigerenzer, Gerd (1999), The recognition heuristic: How ignorance makes us smart. In G. Gigerenzer, P.M. Todd and the ABC Research Group (eds), *Simple Heuristics that Make Us Smart*. Oxford: Oxford University Press, pp. 37–58.

Goncharov, Ivan ([1859]2014), *Oblomov*. London: Alma Classics.

Göteborgs-Posten (2011), "Det här är ju inte klokt." Förre ordföranden för Göteborg Energi förvånad över prisökningen. December 18.

Habermas, Jürgen ([1981]1984), *The Theory of Communicative Action*. Vol. 1: *Reason and the Rationalization of Society*. Boston: Beacon Press.

Hammond, John S., Keeney, Ralph L. and Raiffa, Howard (1998), The hidden traps in decision making. *Harvard Business Review*, September–October.

Harrison, J. Richard and March, James G. (1984), Decision-making and post-decision surprises. *Administrative Science Quarterly*, *29*, pp. 26–42.

Haug, Christoph (2015), What is consensus and how is it achieved in meetings? Four practices of consensus decision-making. In J.A. Allen, N. Lehmann-Willenbrock and S.G. Rogelberg (eds), *The Cambridge Handbook of Meeting Science*. New York, NY: Cambridge University Press, pp. 556–584.

Hedberg, Bo (1976), Mot ett manövrerbart industrisamhälle. In B. Hambraeus and E. Tengström (eds), *Vad kan du och jag göra åt framtiden? Utgångspunkter för en konstruktiv debatt*. Stockholm: Bonniers.

Holmblad Brunsson, Karin (2002), Management or politics – or both? How management by objectives may be managed: A Swedish example. *Financial Accountability & Management*, *18* (2), pp. 189–209.

Holmblad Brunsson, Karin (2011), Den företagsekonomiska etiken. *Økonomistyring & informatik*, *26* (5), pp. 437–452.

Holmblad Brunsson, Karin (2013), *Läran om management: Föreställningar i ett organisationssamhälle*. Lund: Studentlitteratur.

Holub, Miroslav (1977), Brief thoughts on maps. *The Times Literary Supplement*, February 4.

Howard, Andrew (2011), Groupthink and corporate governance reform: Changing the formal and informal decision-making processes of corporate boards. *Southern California Interdisciplinary Law Journal*, *20* (2), pp. 425–457.

Huczynski, Andrzej A. (1993), Explaining the succession of management fads. *The International Journal of Human Resource Management*, *4* (2), pp. 443–463.

Hume, David ([1772]2004), *An Enquiry Concerning Human Understanding*. New York, NY: Barnes and Noble.

Illouz, Eva (2007), *Cold Intimacies. The Making of Emotional Capitalism*. Cambridge: Polity Press.

Jackall, Robert (1988), *Moral Mazes: The World of Corporate Managers*. Oxford: Oxford University Press.

Jacobsson, Bengt (1987), *Kraftsamlingen: Politik och företagande i parallella processer*. Lund: Doxa.

Jacobsson, Bengt, Pierre, Jon and Sundström, Göran (2015), *Governing the Embedded State: The Organizational Dimension of Governance*. Oxford: Oxford University Press.

James, William ([1906]2012), *Pragmatism, A New Name for Some Old Ways of Thinking*. Memphis, TN: Bottom of the Hill Publishing.

Janis, Irving L. (1982), *Groupthink: Psychological Studies of Policy Decisions and Fiascoes*. Boston, MA: Houghton Mifflin.

Jansson, David (1992), *Spelet kring investeringskalkyler: Om den strategiska användningen av det för-givet-tagna*. Stockholm: Norstedts.

Jepperson, Ronald (1991), Institutions, institutional effects, and institutionalism. In W. Powell and P.J. DiMaggio (eds), *The New Institutionalism in Organizational Analysis*. Chicago: Chicago University Press, Chapter 6.

Kahneman, Daniel (2011), *Thinking, Fast and Slow*. London: Penguin Books.

Kahneman, Daniel and Lovallo, Dan (1993), Timid choices and bold forecasts: A cognitive perspective on risk taking. *Management Science*, *39* (1), pp. 17–31.

Kingdon, John W. (1984), *Agendas, Alternatives, and Public Policies*. Boston, MA: Little, Brown and Co.

af Klintberg, Bengt (1986), *Råttan i pizzan: Folksägner i vår tid*. Stockholm: Norstedts.

Krasner, Stephen D. (1999), *Sovereignty: Organized Hypocrisy*. Princeton, NJ: Princeton University Press.

Kreiner, Kristian (2012), Organizational decision mechanisms in architectural competition. In A. Lomi and J.R. Harrison (eds), *The Garbage Can Model of Organizational Choice: Looking Forward at Forty*. Bingley, England: Emerald, pp. 399–430.

La Rochefoucauld, François ([1665]2012), *Maximes et réflexions morales*. Ditzingen: Reclam Philippe Jun.

Langer, Ellen (1975), The illusion of control. *Journal of Personality and Social Psychology*, *32* (2), pp. 311–328.

Levinthal, Daniel A. (2012), From the ivy tower to the c-suite: Garbage can processes and corporate strategic decision making. In A. Lomi and J.R. Harrison (eds), *The Garbage Can Model of Organizational Choice: Looking Forward at Forty*. Bingley, England: Emerald, pp. 349–362.

Levitt, Barbara and March, James G. (1988), Organizational learning. *Annual Review of Sociology*, *14*, pp. 319–340.

Lillpers, Birgitta (2012), *Industriminnen*. Stockholm: Wahlström & Widstrand.

Lindblom, Charles E. (1959), The science of muddling through. *Public Administration Review*, *19*, pp. 79–98.

Lipson, Michael (2007), Peacekeeping: Organized hypocrisy? *European Journal of International Relations*, *13* (1), pp. 5–34.

Luhmann, Niklas (2000), *Organisation und Entscheidung*. Opladen: Westdeutscher Verlag.

Machiavelli, Niccolò ([1513]1992), *The Prince*. Transl. N.H. Tomson. Mineola, NY: Dover Publications.

Mann, Thomas ([1924]1974), *Der Zauberberg*. Hamburg: S. Fischer Verlag.

March, James G. (1978), Bounded rationality, ambiguity and the engineering of choice. *The Bell Journal of Economics*, *9* (2), pp. 587–608.

March, James G. (1987), Ambiguity and accounting: The elusive link between information and decision-making. *Accounting, Organizations and Society*, *12*, pp. 153–168.

March, James G. (1994), *A Primer on Decision Making: How Decisions Happen*. New York, NY: The Free Press.

March, James G. (2010), *The Ambiguities of Experience*. Ithaca, NY: Cornell University Press.

March, James G. and Olsen, Johan P. (1975), The uncertainty of the past: Organizational learning under ambiguity. *European Journal of Political Research*, *3*, pp. 147–171.

March, James G. and Olsen, Johan P. (1989), *Rediscovering Institutions: The Organizational Basis of Politics.* New York, NY: The Free Press.
March, James G. and Simon, Herbert ([1958]1993), *Organizations.* Cambridge, MA: Blackwell.
Masaaki, Imai (1986), *Kaizen: The Key to Japan's Competitive Success.* New York, NY: McGraw-Hill.
Matthew 14:22–33, *KJV.*
Meyer, John W. and Rowan, Brian (1977), Institutional organizations: Formal structure as myth and ceremony. *American Journal of Sociology, 83* (2), pp. 340–363.
Mezias, John M. and Starbuck, William H. (2003), Studying the accuracy of managers' perceptions: A research odyssey. *British Journal of Management, 14*, pp. 3–17.
Musselin, Christine (1996), Organized anarchies: A reconsideration of research strategies. In M. Warglien and M. Masuch (eds), *The Logic of Organizational Disorder.* Berlin: de Gruyter, pp. 55–72.
Nisbett, Richard E. and Ross, Lee (1980), *Human Inference: Strategies and Shortcomings of Social Judgment.* New York, NY: Prentice Hall.
Ocasio, William (1997), Towards an attention-based view of the firm. *Strategic Management Journal, 18*, pp. 187–206.
Ocasio, William (2012), Situated attention, loose and tight coupling, and the garbage can model. In A. Lomi and J.R. Harrison (eds), *The Garbage Can Model of Organizational Choice: Looking Forward at Forty.* Bingley, England: Emerald, pp. 293–318.
Olson, Olov (1996), Forandring i Bergen kommune. In O. Olson and F. Mellemvik (eds), *Regnskap i forandring: Utveckling, spredning och bruk av kommuneregnskap.* Oslo: Cappelen Akademisk forlag.
Oxford English Dictionary (2017), *decision*, n. www.oed.com (accessed January 9, 2017).
Pariser, Eli (2012), *The Filter Bubble: How the Personalized Web is Changing What We Read and What We Think.* London: Penguin Books.
Perrow, Charles (1986), *Complex Organizations: A Critical Essay.* New York, NY: McGraw-Hill.
Pfeffer, Jeffrey and Sutton, Robert I. (2006), *Hard Facts, Dangerous Half-truths and Total Nonsense: Profiting from Evidence-based Management.* Boston, MA: Harvard Business School Press.

Pizzorno, Alessandro (1990), On rationality and democratic choice. In P. Birnbaum and J. Leca (eds), *Individualism: Theories and Methods*. Oxford: Clarendon Press, pp. 141–189.

Porac, Joseph and Rosa, Jost Antonio (1996), In praise of managerial narrow-mindedness. *Journal of Management Inquiry*, 5 (1), pp. 35–42.

Pressman, Jeffrey L. and Wildavsky, Aaron ([1973]1984), *Implementation*. Berkeley, CA: University of California Press.

Proust, Marcel ([1913]2003), *In Search of Lost Time*. Vol. 1: The Way by Swann's (À la recherche du temps perdu. Du côte de chez Swann). London: Penguin Modern Classics.

Røvik, Kjell Arne (2007), Trender og Translasjoner – idéer som former det 21. århundrets organisasjon. Oslo: Universitetsforlaget.

Sahlin-Andersson, Kerstin (1989), *Oklarhetens strategi: Organisering av projektsamarbete*. Lund: Studentlitteratur.

Saint Paul, 1 Corinthians 13:9–12, *KJV*.

Scapens, Robert W. (1985), *Management Accounting: A Review of Contemporary Developments*. London: Macmillan.

Schwartz, Norbert (2000), Emotion, cognition, and decision making. *Cognition and Emotion*, 14 (4), pp. 433–440.

Second Opinion (2014), Göteborg Energis vd: Snedvriden konkurrens på biogasmarknaded. http://second-opinion.se (accessed February 6, 2017).

Sevón, Guje (1996), Organizational imitation in identity transformation. In B. Czarniawska and G. Sevón (eds), *Translating Organizational Change*. Berlin: de Gruyter, pp. 49–68.

Shakespeare, William (ca [1599]1960), Hamlet, Prince of Denmark. In *William Shakespeare, The Complete Works*. London: Collins, pp. 1028–1072.

Shapira, Zur (2008), On the implications of behavioral decision theory for managerial decision making: Contributions and challenges. In G.P. Hodgkinson and W.H. Starbuck (eds), *The Oxford Handbook of Organizational Decision Making*. Oxford: Oxford University Press, pp. 287–304.

Shklar, Judith N. (1984), *Ordinary Vices*. Cambridge, MA: Harvard University Press.

Simon, Herbert (1955), A behavioral model of rational choice. *The Quarterly Journal of Economics*, 69 (1), pp. 99–118.

Simon, Herbert ([1957]1965), *Administrative Behavior: A Study of Decision-making Processes in Administrative Organization*. New York, NY: The Free Press.

112   *Decisions*

Simon, Herbert (1987), Making management decisions: The role of intuition and emotion. *Academy of Management Executive*, February, pp. 57–64.

Simonson, Itamar (1989), Choice based on reasons: The case of attraction and compromise effects. *Journal of Consumer Research*, *16*, pp. 158–174.

Sims, Ronald R. (1992), Linking groupthink to unethical behavior in organizations. *Journal of Business Ethics*, *11* (9), pp. 651–662.

SOU (2005:104), *Sverige och tsunamin: Granskning och förslag*. Huvudrapport från 2005 års katastrofkommission. Stockholm: Fritzes.

Stanovich, Keith E. and West, Richard F. (2000), Individual differences in reasoning: Implications for the rationality debate? *Behavioral and Brain Science*, *23* (5), pp. 645–726.

Staw, Barry M. and Ross, Jerry (1987), Behavior in escalation situations: Antecedents, prototypes, and solutions. *Research in Organizational Behavior*, *9*, pp. 39–78.

Stein, Johan (1999), Ledarskap och professionalisering. In S.-E. Sjöstrand, J. Sandberg and M. Tyrstrup (eds), *Osynlig företagsledning*. Lund: Studentlitteratur.

Strang, David and Meyer, John W. (1993), Institutional conditions for diffusion. *Theory and Society*, *22*, pp. 487–511.

Swieringa, Robert J. and Weick, Karl E. (1987), Management accounting and action. *Accounting, Organizations and Society*, *12* (3), pp. 293–308.

Tamm Hallström, Kristina (2004), *Organizing International Standardization – ISO and the IASC in Quest of Authority*. Cheltenham, UK and Northampton, MA, USA: Edward Elgar Publishing.

Tarschys, Daniel (2006), Mål utan mening? Om ordstyrning i landet där allt är prioriterat. In M. Lemne (ed.), *Förvaltningens byggstenar*. Statskontorets småskrifter 2006:1. Stockholm: Statskontoret.

Tengblad, Stefan (2000), *Verkställande direktörer i arbete*. GRI-rapport 2000:11. Göteborg: Göteborgs universitet.

Thaler, Richard H. and Sunstein, Cass R. (2008), *Nudge: Improving Decisions about Health, Wealth and Happiness*. London: Penguin Books.

The Guardian (2016), Four of world's biggest cities to ban diesel cars from their centres. https://www.theguardian.com/

environment/2016/dec/02/four-of-worlds-biggest-cities-to-ban-diesel-cars-from-their-centres (accessed August 30, 2017).

Tolstoy, Leo ([1869]2017), *War and Peace*. London: Penguin Classics.

Tversky, Amos and Kahneman, Daniel (1986), Rational choice and the framing of decisions. *Journal of Business, 59* (4), pp. 251–278.

Veyne, Paul (1983), *Les grecs ont-ils cru à leur mythes? Essai sur l'imagination constituante*. Paris: Éditions de Seuil.

Walgenbach, Peter and Hegele, Cornelia (2001), What can an apple learn from an orange? Or: What do companies like benchmarking for? *Organization, 8* (1), pp. 121–144.

Weber, Max ([1924]1964), *The Theory of Social and Economic Organization* (Wirtschaft und Gesellschaft, I). New York, NY: The Free Press.

Weick, Karl E. (1976), Educational organizations as loosely coupled systems. *Administrative Science Quarterly, 21*, pp. 1–19.

Weick, Karl E. (1995), *Sensemaking in Organizations*. Thousand Oaks, CA: Sage Publications.

Weick, Karl E. (1996), Drop your tools: An allegory for organizational studies. *Administrative Science Quarterly, 41*, pp. 301–313.

Weick, Karl E. (2007), Drop your tools: On reconfiguration management education. *Journal of Management Education, 31* (1), pp. 5–16.

Weick, Karl E., Sutcliffe, Kathleen M. and Obstfeld, David (2005), Organizing and the process of sensemaking. *Organization Science, 16* (4), pp. 409–421.

Weil, Simone (1957), *Attente de Dieu*. Paris: La Colombe.

Wildavsky, Aaron (1975), *Budgeting: A Comparative Theory of Budgetary Processes*. Boston, MA: Little, Brown and Co.

Wren, Daniel A. (2005), *The History of Management Thought*. London: Wiley.

YouTube (2013a), Interview with the Swedish King och Silvia Sommerlath. February 11, 1976 (retrieved November 12, 2013).

YouTube (2013b), Crown Princess Victoria and Daniel Westling are engaged. February 24, 2009 (retrieved November 12, 2013).

Zern, Leif (2012), *Kaddish på motorcykel*. Stockholm: Bonniers.

Index